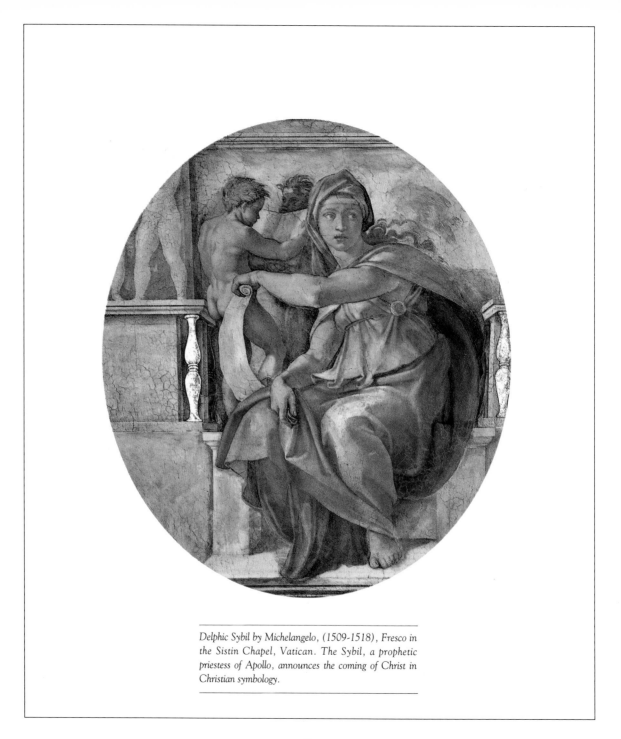

Delphic Sybil by Michelangelo, (1509-1518), Fresco in the Sistin Chapel, Vatican. The Sybil, a prophetic priestess of Apollo, announces the coming of Christ in Christian symbology.

THE SONG OF EVE

Mythology and Symbols of the Goddess

MANUELA
DUNN MASCETTI

Introduction by
Jennifer Woolger, M.A. and Roger Woolger, Ph.D.

A Fireside Book

Published by Simon & Schuster Inc.

New York London Toronto Sydney Tokyo Singapore

F

FIRESIDE
Simon & Schuster Building
Rockefeller Center
1230 Avenue of the Americas
New York, New York 10020

Designed by Magda Valine
Typesetting and computer graphics by Simonetta Castelli, Florence

The Song of Eve was produced by Labyrinth Publishing S. A., Switzerland
Printed and bound in Barcelona, Spain by Cronion S. A.
Color separation by Photochromo Finar, S. A., Spain
Typeset at MicroPRINT, via Pacini 49 / 51 – Florence, Italy

1   3   5   7   9   10   8   6   4   2

Library of Congress Cataloging in Publication Data
Mascetti, Manuela Dunn.
    The song of Eve / Manuela Dunn Mascetti.
        p.   cm.
    "A Fireside book."
    ISBN 0–671–68890–1
    1. Goddesses   2. Feminism––Religious aspects.   3. Mythology–
–Psychological aspects.   I. Title.
BL473.5.M33 1990
291.2'114––dc20   90–33179
                                                                    CIP

Contents

Introduction by:

Jennifer Barker Woolger M.A. and Roger Woolger Ph.D.,
authors of "The Goddess Within".

  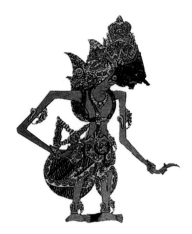

As the universal principal of paradox, the Goddess is the "faceless presence met in ordinary worldly affairs" and "the riddle no man could aspire to solve lest he lose his life and return to her womb." She is the Mother and the Untouched Maiden. In times of peace and harmony, She is the Bestower of all that is good and gracious. But when turmoil and war shake the earth and Her help is sincerely called upon, She comes to save the world from ruin. Perhaps this is one reason why She is coming so powerfully to consciousness in woman and man throughout the Christian, Western world: we know ourselves to be in serious trouble in the unnatural and violent world that we have created.

But we must go deeper to understand the fascination of the Great Goddess in her many forms. Not simply a divinity, She is a unified multiplicity, a one-ness born from the visible and transcendent. Hers is the voice that affirms us in our infinite variety: the attitude of tolerance born of endless creation and destruction and recreation. And Hers is the voice of the feminine body and of the earth itself, observed in mountains, the rolling countryside and the seas. The rocks of the earth are Her bones, and the grasses Her flowing hair. The old wisdom of farmers is that mowing hay is a way to comb the Mother's hair.

Furthermore, the Goddess bestows upon us the gift of transformation. With Her life-restoring energy, She can penetrate the human soul and heart to bring about miraculous changes. Embodying Her, we become Her.

It has been more than 2,000 years since the Goddess was recognized as the primary spiritual force on earth. The idea of a single Sky Father god was still relatively new when the carpenter's son was born to give

rise to Gnosticism, the Roman Church, Protestantism and all the contemporary, fundamentalist Christian churches. Today, when violence against women and girl children is epidemic and the toxic destruction of the earth is at an extreme turning point, the recognition of the transformative power of the Goddess is re-emerging to show us ways out of our self-created Hell.

Myths and stories have been sung and told since time before time. Myths, and the universal, unifying principals they contain form the loom on which the fabric of a family, tribe or nation is woven. They define the collective wisdom of a people derived from the direct physical experience of life. They describe what we can expect from life in terms of the natural cycles of youth, maturity and old age; cycles observed both inwardly and in the lunar and seasonal cycles of the natural world. Myths of the Goddess are some of the most ancient of stories and have the profound effect of connecting us in an unbroken chain from grandmother to mother to daughter.

Never before in our human history have the challenges and opportunities been so great for women. The radical political and social changes worldwide have brought about a disintegration of familiar, traditional roles for women, forcing them out of their homes and off their farms to find means of survival in cities. And never before have so many women reached the maturity of their post-childbearing years in good health, with the freedom and resources to explore the nature of themselves and to influence the social and political structures around them. It is in this context that the Goddess in her guises is re-emerging. All of the Goddesses have stories to tell, contributions to make and wisdom to share. It is cause for rejoicing.

Author's Introduction

THE Song of Eve is the song of all women. Its first chant must have sounded more centuries ago than we can count and its melody has been heard constantly throughout all creeds and beliefs of humanity, sometimes lost in the complexities of reason, organized religion or patriarchy, but always surfacing again to be picked up by new voices.

The women of this century have surfaced from a long "underground" period of suppression and servitude to a social system that imagined they were of secondary importance. The length of time that women have been suppressed has been so long that perhaps they have even forgotten their own abilities to change. Still today they are often choosing to identify with the male methods – thoughtful, reasonable and linear – whereas there is much to show us that more natural approaches exist to be discovered and the very fact that there is currently so much written material available for the feminine mind seems to show her unstoppable power to find a greater freedom.

This book is a lavish study of the Goddess in all her colors and finery. The substance of the study is to bring words and illustrations together as a sort of tapestry of beauty so that the reader can sample the contents through more than simply the intellect, and thereby appreciate the power of femininity with more than one sense. In the past, the Song of Eve was not only written, it was also sung, danced, and painted. It was more often than not memorized and passed on through word of mouth, through story telling and all forms of sensual representation. So why would we here wish to do any different?

The Goddess was the illogical coexistence of opposing forces; the faceless presence met in ordinary worldly affairs and in the untrodden paths of the unknown. The cult of the Goddess was an all encompassing one which gave way to the male monotheistic religions of the present day.

The presence of the Goddess in today's Western culture no longer remains as a cult dominating the patterns of life and death, but as a mysterious power which we rarely trust and know little about. Her veiled figure has remained an existential mystery since the earliest cultures through to most recent history. She was the riddle no man could aspire to solve, lest he lost his life and returned to her womb: mother of all mankind, animals and plants; earth and sky; death and rebirth; saint and whore; light and dark; child and crone; peace and war; enticing and rejecting.

As the pendulum of life swings toward the center of its arched path, we find ourselves at a time in history where we need to re-consider who we were in order to understand who we are now, and as humanity re-dimensions itself, the old and the new merge together.

In the last years, there has been a considerable interest in returning to the earth, to our roots. We are looking at our lives from a different perspective; wo-

men, in particular, seem more and more drawn to an attitude that respects rather than annihilates life. Health foods, natural life styles, the New Age, life function through natural resources – these are some of the outer manifestation.

Behind the passion for the "esoteric," the "natural," there is a trend of far greater significance: a return to the ways of the Goddess, to the mysteries of an age where the magic of women dominated the temporal as well as the spiritual plains.

This book is an illustration of the very different dimensions and aspects of the Goddess; not a journey through time and its changes, but a table laid for a rich banquet in which we may see the Goddesses at work in their many guises, guises that are suddenly recognizable in each of our lives and actions, providing an exciting and new form of identification which in turn will give understanding so that the Song of Eve may be sung once again.

CHAPTER ONE:

The Archetypes of the Goddess –
Myths of the Feminine

The Way we Are – The Physiology of Myth – The Archetypal Biography of
Woman – A Goddess for Every Woman – The Archetype of the Virgin – The
Archetype of the Creator and Destroyer – The Archetype of the Lover /
Seductress – The Archetype of the Mother – The Archetype of the Priestess
and Wise Woman – The Archetype of the Muse

The Way we Are

THE EMPHASIS OF MODERN education lies in the flowering of the mind. We probe and question every detail, every aspect of ourselves and the world that surrounds us, in an attempt one day to understand. The process, however, is far from being the innocent inquiry of the child or of the true saint, for everything around us exists as evidence of the system's success: a worthy career, a nobility of spirit, social respectability. Even the trees, the soil and its fruits are good, solid things. Things that matter. But still we remain empty, spiritless, worthless, as if we lived in a world of shadows. Why ?

In this quest for understanding with its ever growing avenues of complexity, we have fallen into the rapture of constantly asking. The truth is we already know the answer, an answer which is deeply rooted in our past, shaping our reality every day of our lives, even though we may not always be aware of it. For this is mythology – the sound of the world, the life and spirit that we so much long to gain again. For mythology is a language invented by man to speak on the instinctual plane, where answers are not known, but felt with a great impact.

The intention of this book is to reveal through text and pictures the mythology of the Goddess and the archetypes that revolve around it touching the core of every woman.

Mythology is the unfolding of the immemorial and traditional material in which tales of Gods, Goddesses and god-like beings, heroic battles and journeys to the Underworld are contained. Far from being static material, it moves, transforms and speaks to us in pictures, evoking particular feelings [1]. It has, metaphorically, a sound of its own. A torrent of pictures streams out, like music, from the myths of the Goddess. What they describe in tales are the most intimate moments of a woman's life, like falling in love or childbirth, and justice is done to the myths if they are allowed to utter, as if in a song, their own unique meaning. Like music, mythology is an appropriate art for the expression of feelings and the movements of the heart. We cannot effectively describe a mythological tale in precise terms, for in so doing we strip it of its "living" qualities. It dies in the grasping act of thoughtful consideration.

For those within whose lands mythology is indigenous, it is not only sung as the music of creation, but actually lived. Gods, Goddesses, heroes as well as mortal men and women, take a step back before any action, like a toreador honoring his bull before the death stroke, like a wave arrests its force before crashing ashore. In these moments silence speaks and its voice is deeply satisfying for it has the ring of truth.

Bronislaw Malinowski, a field-worker who spent many years amongst the indigenous populations of the Trobriand Islands in the South Pacific, explains in his paper *Myth in Primitive Psychology* [2] his experience of a "living mythology":

Rock painting from the Bovidian period depicting rams and goats, Tassili (Iheren).

"The myth in a primitive society, i.e. in its original living form, is not a mere tale told but a reality lived. It is not in the nature of an invention such as we read in our novels today, but living reality, believed to have occurred in primordial times and to be influencing ever afterwards the world and the destinies of men. ... These stories are not kept alive by vain curiosity, neither as tales that have been invented nor again as tales that are true. For the natives on the contrary they are the assertion of an original, greater, and more important reality through which the present life, fate, and work of mankind are governed, and the knowledge of which provides men on the one hand with motives for ritual and moral acts, on the other for directions for their performance."

Mythology speaks to us in symbols, that is, in terms or pictures that may be familiar to us in everyday life which nevertheless possess, in the mythological context, specific connotations in addition to conventional and obvious meanings. A mythological symbol implies something hidden, unknown, difficult to describe in the temporal language. A common example would be that of the wheel or the cross, objects used all over the world, which may assume a symbolic significance, given the right circumstances. Mythological symbolism is more often beyond the reach of rational understanding, representing concepts that move our emotions in a rapture of psychological force. Our common use of symbolic language to describe "the indescribable," is evidence enough of man's unconscious

tendency to create symbolic mythology [3].

It is only very recently that the empirical science of psychology has developed as a mirror to man's inner world. The psychological experience has two main facets: reality which exists outside us and our perception of it which is imprinted as a psychic event. We have come to learn over the last century that our psyche never comprehends anything fully nor perceives anything completely. The world, with its events and objects, is not contained but *translated*, into the realm of the mind. This translation, however, happens on both conscious and unconscious levels. There may be events which we do not recollect consciously, but somehow sub-consciously as they emerge in moments of intuition, deep thought, or dreams.

There may be other events that have been "censored" deliberately so that their memory, which may carry negative feelings of shame or guilt, may not haunt us. These memories can again be brought to consciousness during hypnosis or in dreams. The unconscious or sub-conscious reveals its contents to the conscious in the form of symbols and the process is spontaneous and common to all men and women.

Mythology is a symbolic language which can be compared with this intuitive, sub-conscious level of memory, and one that reveals the contents of the collective rather than personal unconscious.

The Physiology of Myth

PRIMITIVE man, whose consciousness appears to be at a different level of development from our own, feels that his soul not only dwells within his body, but also with the trees, animals, stars, thunder and all other natural phenomena of his outdoor world. The psychic identity of a man with a tree, for instance, might be so strong that when the tree is cut the man falls seriously ill, as if he also was to die. This *mystical participation* (*) with the world is alien to modern man, which perhaps explains why we cannot fully comprehend that the destruction of rain forests is the destruction and alienation also of indigenous populations.

Whether our consciousness is primitive or modern, the fact remains that there are still aspects of ourselves which are obscured from reason. These aspects nevertheless influence us on a profound level. We need therefore to analyze this point in order to grasp the extent of the force produced in us by the symbols and mythologies universal to mankind.

Certain imprints, deriving from the direct physical experience of life such as day and night, above and

* 'mystical participation' is a term coined by the French ethnologist Lucien Levy-Bruehl.

below, cold and hot, are impressed upon the nervous system in the period between birth and death and many of these are the source of our most widely known mythological images. The responses of pleasure and fear to the experience of the world, for instance, shape our mode of being so profoundly that they are recorded in mythology as the foundation of our lives [4].

The forces that maintain life on earth and that structure our own existence as well as the existence of every star, animal and plant in the world as we know it, form the roots of cosmic mythology, the myths reflecting the laws that govern us. The force of gravity works continuously on every aspect of natural and human affairs and has fundamentally conditioned the form of the body and its organs. The pull toward the earth appears in mythological tales as a mysterious force that attracts man to the lower world and hinders elevation to a higher state.

The daily alternation of day and night has a powerful influence on man's physical existence. At night the world sleeps and the mind plunges into the realm of the dream experience. Upon waking, doubt, that flickering light that accompanies man throughout his journey, may reveal the fickleness of reality and the dream may seem still more real. In the life of Chuang Tzu we find one of the most beautiful incidents that explains the duality of dream and waking life, the polarity between reality and non-reality.

Left: Kalanala yantra, symbolizing the Fire of Doom, merging Spirit with Pure Wisdom. Rajastan, 18th century, gouache on paper. Right: Contemporary vision of Kali as "preserver." Colored pencils on paper, Priya Mookerjee, New York.

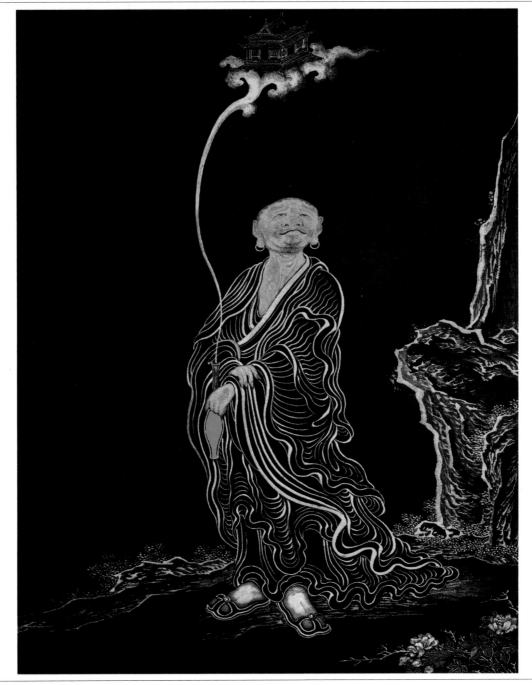

Left: The second disciple of Buddha, who created a pearly palace from a vase simply by snapping his fingers. The palace symbolizes Nirvana, the awakening from the dream. Right: The laughing monks of Zen.

One morning Chuang Tzu was sitting in bed and feeling very sad. Sadness was against his nature and teaching. His disciples gathered around him and were very worried. One disciple plucked up enough courage to ask Chuang Tzu if there was anything wrong. The master replied that in the night he had dreamed he was a butterfly. The disciples laughed and reassured him that it was only a dream and that he need not be sad. The master asked them to listen to the whole story. A strange idea had arisen in his heart; if Chuang Tzu could become a butterfly in his dream, why could not a butterfly become Chuang Tzu in her dream? Who was awake and who dreaming – Chuang Tzu or the butterfly – at this moment? The master was inquiring into the problem of identity. Was he Chuang Tzu dreaming of being a butterfly in sleep or was he a butterfly living a dream of being Chuang Tzu?

In the dream, the sense of time and identity are lost; one is pulled and torn by the senses and meets characters unknown in reality, while objects take on a life of their own. The world of myth is saturated by the experience of dream. The creation myths are often set in a dream-like stage, where time and form are not yet created.

Dawn is the time of awakening, when the dark forces of the night are dispersed and a new day begins. At this time animals are at their most choral while primary activities such as cleaning and feeding take place. In mythology, the freshness of dawn is the time of revelation, when heroes find the answer to their search and new life is created.

The solar star is the master of daytime; its positive, fiery force is often likened to the dominating strength of the father; its domains of power are the growing of crops and the nurturing of the earth. All animals possess an internal clock which measures the position of the sun in the sky during the day and also within the yearly arch. The internal clock regulates feeding times and amounts, sleeping times and migratory and hibernation cycles, as well as mating periods.

We have not entirely forgotten how to measure our lives by the regulating internal sun clock. Despite the clocks that tell us when things should be done, we obey our own internal rhythm for matters of natural life. During sleep the heartbeat and blood circulation slow down, giving the body a rest. We briefly emerge from sleep as the sun rises and then perhaps return to sleep for a few hours more. Our feeding cycles are altered by the seasons.

As early in history as we are able to trace, man has erected temples, such as the famous Stonehenge, to both worship and study the sun, the ruler of life on earth. The brightness of the sun is found as symbol in mythologies throughout the world of positive, clear wisdom and the capacity to illuminate mankind's world.

In direct contrast to the sun, the moon rises every night to remind us of the mysterious in ordinary reality. As the sunlight is masculine, aggressive, violent and passionate, moonlight is feminine, soft, tender, receptive, loving.

In Racine's version of the Greek tragedy of Phaedra,

royal wife to Theseus and step-mother to Hyppolitus, Phaedra is haunted by the incestuous desire to love Hyppolitus. She dares confess her obsession to no one, and lives in the shadows of her palace for fear that the rays of the sun might find her and reveal her love. The sun is her persecutor and only in the moonlight does she appear in the open and chant her desire to the soft night breeze. In poetry and in the stories of mythology sunlight and moonlight are in direct opposition and in this book the theme will be found again and again as the Goddesses of the night unfold their mysteries.

Normal, everyday phenomena such as gravity forces, night and day, the turning of the seasons, take on a grander scale when placed within mythology. Goddesses, in particular, symbolize the polarities of above and below, light and dark, confidence and fear, death and resurrection. The elements of changeless change in our universe are to be found in myth as symbols of the Goddess. The moon, for instance, with the likeness of its phases to the menstrual cycle and to the three ages of woman (new moon representing the virgin, full moon representing the fully flowered woman and the waning moon symbolizing the wise woman) finds a special place in the mythology and symbols of the Goddess. A full moon night is the most feminine night of all. Dogs bark, men become moon-struck, and the all-powerful energy of the sun transforms into a cool, mysterious power in an alchemical process that is symbolically significant. Since our earliest known civilizations women revered the moon as the protector of their mysteries and, among other functions, as giver of fertility. Women of primitive tribes such as the Greenlanders will not look at the moon and will not sleep on their backs without first rubbing spittle on their stomachs in order to prevent pregnancy from the moon. The Nigerians believe that no husband is needed for procreation, as the Great Moon Mother sends the Moon Bird to the earth to bring babies to the women.[5]

There is an old Sanskrit legend to the effect that, after making man, the Creator took the rotundity of the moon, the curves of the creeper, the lightness of leaves, the weeping of the clouds, the cruelty of the tiger, the soft flow of fire, the coldness of the snows, and the chattering of the jays, and made woman, and presented her to man. After three days the man came and said to the Almighty, "This woman you have given me chatters constantly, never leaves me alone, requires much attention, takes all my time, cries about nothing and is always idle. I want you to take her back." So the Almighty took her back. But pretty soon the man came back and said, "She used to dance and sing, and she looked at me out of the corner of her eye, and she loved to play; she clung to me when she was afraid, her laughter was like music, and she was beautiful to look upon. Give her back to me again." So the Almighty gave her back to him again. But three days later he brought her back again and asked the Almighty to keep her. "No," said the Lord, "you will not live with her, and you cannot live without her. You have to get along the best you can." [6]

Page 20: Encounter between the contrasting masculine and feminine principles (sun and moon). Miniature from the alchemical treatise Aurora consurgens (14th-15th century). Zurich, Central Library.
Page 21: The playfulness of woman has been mystified in a Sanskrit legend which tells of the endless game between man and woman.
Page 22: "Full Moon" by M. Valine.

To be a woman is certainly a question of a psychology firmly rooted in the physiology of the female body. In the last few decades, women have been psychologically nearer the male aggressive mentality because certain basic rules of their existence needed to be altered, with force, within the framework of the society in which we live. However, to be truly womanly is to be receptive in a religious sense. Man reaches this state when he becomes drunk with God – he becomes, psychologically, as receptive as a woman, and this is the great transformation that we call enlightenment.

Jesus's offering of the other cheek was fundamentally a teaching of "resist not evil" – a total receptivity to existence and its offerings. The great Sufi poet Jalaluddin Rumi whispers similar sentiments in one of his poems.

> *"I am filled with you.*
> *Skin, blood, bone, brain, and soul.*
> *There is no room for lack of trust, or trust.*
> *Nothing in this existence, but that existence."* [7]

Both these mystics, in their different ways, were utterly drunk with the divine and their terms of address for it were the intimate "father" for Jesus and the "beloved" for Rumi.

Women are drunk with the same receptivity and moreover it is their natural state – a state which stems from the capacity to create life and a state also intimately connected with the roots of mythology. We have an opportunity therefore to learn the mythological tales representing fundamental aspects of the female psyche, searching into the links between the female body and its functions and the mythology of the Goddess with its symbols, to rediscover an integrity which is proper only to womanhood and that can on no account be compared with a male *Weltanschauung*. [8]

The Archetypal Biography of Woman

Woman is the creator of the universe,
the universe is her form;
woman is the foundation of the world,
she is the true form of the body.
Whatever form she takes,
Whether the form of a man or a woman,
is the superior form.
In woman is the form of all things,
of all that lives and moves in the world.
There is no jewel rarer than woman,
no condition superior to that of a woman.
There is not, nor has been, nor will be
any destiny to equal that of a woman;
there is no kingdom, no wealth
to be compared with a woman;
there is not, nor has been, nor will be
any holy place like unto a woman.
There is no prayer to equal a woman.
There is not, nor has been, nor will be
any yoga to compare with a woman,
no mystical formula nor ascetism
to match a woman.
There are not, nor have been, nor will be
any riches more valuable than woman.
Saktisangama Tantra.[9]

Venus by Titian. Gallerie Uffizi, Florence.

The female physiological make-up has greater significance in the context of mythology than we might imagine. Apart from personal experiences, which are recorded within the *personal* unconscious, there is a range of inborn responses to life which are stored within the *collective* unconscious. These are modes of behavior which are more or less the same in all individuals. The contents of the collective unconscious are called archetypes and one form of their conscious expression is within the frame of mythology. Experiences that mark profoundly the life of a woman, such as the menstrual cycle, pregnancy, birth and menopause, produce a different impact in each individual and are therefore recorded differently in the personal unconscious. On a deeper level, however, these are experiences shared by all women throughout the ages and as such they form a common ground within the collective unconscious. The mythology of the Goddess is the outward expression of the archetypes of the feminine – it tells of the different experiences lived throughout our lives. Traditionally, woman has been seen to undergo three different stages of maturity which are the young woman, the fully flowered woman and the wise older woman. Unique psychological and physical experiences characterize each stage, giving form to the six archetypes belonging to the mythology of the Goddess. Each one of the archetypes expressed in the myths of the Goddess operates in the life of every woman by producing a direct impact upon her psychology. Understanding mythology is understanding the reflection produced by the archetype in the mirror of our self. A small detail of our behavior, for instance, may assume greater significance and reveal the key to a puzzle we were trying to solve for a long time when seen through a myth. The fluidity of the mythology of the Goddess makes it possible for every woman to recognize her own experiences and characteristics within its context, tracing the pathway to our own true self.

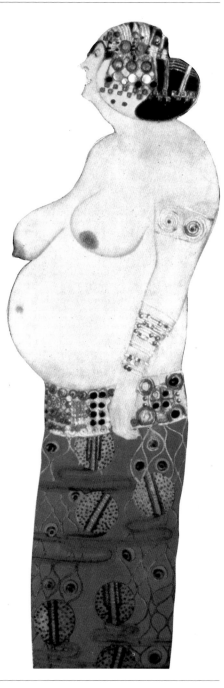

A Goddess for Every Woman

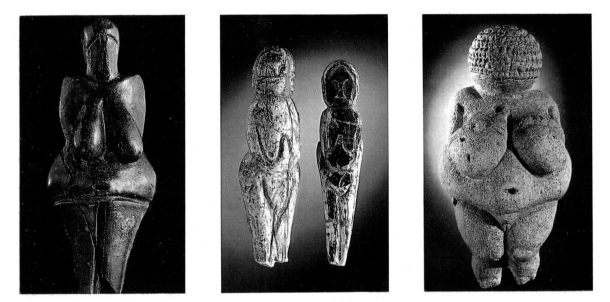

IN the past, Goddesses were a lively part of the social and religious structure of an ethnic group. Since the Upper Paleolithic, which can loosely be defined as the dawn of mankind, systems of temporal notations based on the observation of the phases of the moon, with its course linked to the menstrual cycle, and traces of ritual objects used in female religious ceremonies, tell us of the strong, pervading presence of a female deity.[10] The agrarian cultures which settled, almost eleven thousand years ago, in the Mesopotamic Fertile Crescent, developed a cosmic religion which involved the constant and periodic renewal of life with the Mother Goddess as the focus of worship. The earth was perceived as mother and all animals and plants and men were her children and subject to her laws. The mystery of female sexuality, of parthenogenesis, of the association of the female cycle with the rhythm of the moon, of the earth seen as the womb, of the death of the seed for creation, are all fundamental motifs of the mythology of the Mother Goddess. The primitive villages were centered around the place of prayers and rituals, in the same way as life is metaphorically centered around the source of creation, the womb. The primordial Goddess was thus one, encompassing all forces of life, death and rebirth within her figure. All women were her priestesses, devoted to her will and the worldly manifestations of her power and magic.

It is with the advent of the Greek culture, highly sophisticated and greatly differentiated in comparison with the Mesopotamic civilizations, that we can best understand the influence of the Goddess in the everyday life of a woman. The religion of ancient Greece

Left: Early representations of the Mother Goddess. Clockwise: Oldest known baked clay figurine, 25,000 years, from Dolni Vestonice, Moravian Museum, c. 520 BC. – 15,000-year-old Ivory figurines, from Malta, Siberia, Hermitage Museum – Limestone Venus of Willendorf, Natural History Museum, Vienna, Austria. Right: Kore, Athens, National Archaeological Museum. The Kore represents the Maiden in Greek Mythology.

reflected the patriarchal ideas of its social structure. The one powerful Goddess was no longer the main focus of worship, for male gods were also incorporated within the rich Greek pantheon. Many Goddesses took the form of the primordial Goddess, each one representing one of the aspects of the one and only. The main structure of Greek myth was profoundly influenced by the presence of the Goddesses: they represented the home and the bond of woman to man, the natural life of animals, plants and mankind, the courage in affirmation, fertility and erotic love. Western thought is a direct inheritance and elaboration of classical Greek philosophy and religious structure. The archetypes represented by the Goddesses of the Hellenic pantheon are therefore familiar to our way of thinking and of perceiving reality. Women living in those times saw their own existence in the context of the Goddesses. They worshipped and sought the counsel of the Goddess in all aspects of their daily lives. They prayed to Aphrodite if they wanted to seduce a man; they called on Hestia's help in order to make a house into a home with the warmth of a hearth. The Goddesses genuinely influenced their lives and homage was rendered to them for divine anger would result from the dissatisfaction of the Goddesses.

For contemporary women, the Goddesses exist as psychological archetypes. No longer part of a religious and social structure, the Goddess resides within each woman's heart. The myths of the feminine are a vehicle for the understanding of the archetypes that are at work within our psychology and personality, for they delineate the psychological patterns influencing us.

Each woman may feel affinity with one or more Goddesses, depending on interacting elements such as family, background, conditions and predisposition to change.

The experiences of both physical and psychological growth are recorded in the collective unconscious in the form of archetypes. In the following chapters, therefore, we will see how the myths and their Goddesses can work in our everyday lives.

The Archetype of the Virgin

THE first archetype to be considered stems directly from the experience of every girl at the age when she begins to recognize that she is no longer a child, but a woman. This very tender moment is characterized by pensive moods, lost and languid looks, sudden changes of will, as if the whole body and psyche were framed within a chrysalid from which there is no escape except through the inevitable transformation.

From the age of eleven to fourteen years, we see the "young virgin" as she is portrayed in mythology, with budding breasts and rounded, yet boyish contours inspiring a particular kind of sexual desire. Her sexuality is present in her eyes and movements, but it is fugitive in her actions, both attracting and repelling in a game of subtle, often

innocent, seduction. The young virgin lives on the borderline of sainthood and sin, her body is pure and untouched and yet it expresses the force of an unbroken wave of sexual passion, of the longing for unity with a man and with life seen through the new veil of love.

Such a creature inspires the most chaste of romantic men to burst into a burning passion that has filled page upon page of poetry and romantic literature, her silhouette defining the contours of the archetypal virgin.

She is the character *Beauty*, the young girl of unselfish goodness, who enters into a bond with a grown man, dangerously close to her in moral terms – her father – in the fable "Beauty and the Beast."

Beauty, the youngest of four daughters, became her father's favorite because of her unselfish goodness. When she asks her father only for a white rose, instead of the more costly presents demanded by her sisters, she is aware only of her inner sincerity of feeling. She does not know that she is about to endanger her father's life and her ideal relation with him. For he steals the white rose from the enchanted garden of Beast, who is stirred to anger by the theft and requires him to return in three months for his punishment (presumably death).

Beauty insists upon taking her father's punishment and returns after three months to the enchanted castle. There she is given a beautiful room where she has no worries and nothing to fear except the occasional visit

from Beast, who repeatedly comes to ask her if she will some day marry him. She always refuses. Then, seeing in a magic mirror her father lying ill, she begs Beast to allow her to return to comfort him, promising to return in a week. Beast tells her that he will die if she deserts him, but she may go for a week.

At home, her radiant presence brings joy to her father and envy to her sisters, who plot to detain her longer than her promised stay. At length she dreams that Beast is dying of despair. So, realizing that she has outstayed her time, she returns to resuscitate him. Quite forgetting the dying Beast's ugliness, Beauty ministers to him. He tells her that he was unable to live without her, and that he will die happy now that she has returned. But Beauty realizes that she cannot live without Beast, for she has fallen in love with him. She tells him so and promises to be his wife if only he will not die.

At this the castle is filled with a blaze of light and the sound of music, and Beast disappears. In his place stands a handsome prince, who tells Beauty that he had been enchanted by a witch and turned into the Beast. The spell was ordained to last until a beautiful girl should love Beast for his goodness alone.

Above: "The End of the Monster" by Picasso. In the legend "Beauty and the Beast," Beauty ends the spell that kept the Prince captive in the form of Beast through the power of true love.

Left: "The Beggar Maid" by Sir Edward Burne-Jones. The imagination of painters and poets has been fired for centuries by the archetypal virgin. Right: Kali, the creator and destroyer, sits on her spouse's body creating new life through sexual union and destroying it at the same time by severing heads. The stream depicted in the image represents the river of life, which streams from her dualistic actions.

The archetype of the Virgin is active in a young woman, influencing her on a deeply psychological level. The experience of the passage from childhood to womanhood was, in ancient times, celebrated with rituals, and although this is not any longer so today, the events of this transition are not forgotten by most young women. Nothing that is lived and experienced is ever wiped from our unconscious and especially not such an event as this. A fully matured woman may, thus, have retained some of the traits represented by the archetype of the young virgin, the memory of which can trigger all manner of feelings later in life.

The virgin in mythology does not necessarily appear as young in her psychology in the way that a true young girl might be. She may be the powerful Amazon, a woman who has chosen to lead her life on her own, a companion to man without her relationship to him being a sexual one. The innocence and purity of the virgin may be highlighted, as in the Virgin Mary who conceived and gave birth to Christ without fault. We must analyze with great intelligence the qualities and symbols in an archetypal myth, in order to find some indicators to the psychology of a woman. In the past, men have been the analysts, often entangling their own natural feelings about women with the subtler significance of a myth which perhaps they cannot so easily understand from the female point of view. A woman must understand the significance herself and reveal herself to the world, because no man is going to do it for her.

If we unravel the symbolism of the tale, we see that Beauty begs to be rescued from an exclusively virtuous and unreal love. Her unconscious intention puts her father and then herself in the power of a principle that expresses not goodness alone, but cruelty and kindness combined. In other words, Beauty innocently trusts in a father who is unable to give her the pure white rose of his feeling without awakening the erotic fury of the Beast. It is not until Beauty awakens to the sexual element present in her original wish and to the fear of incest which had repressed it, that she acknowledges her true response to sexuality as a woman.

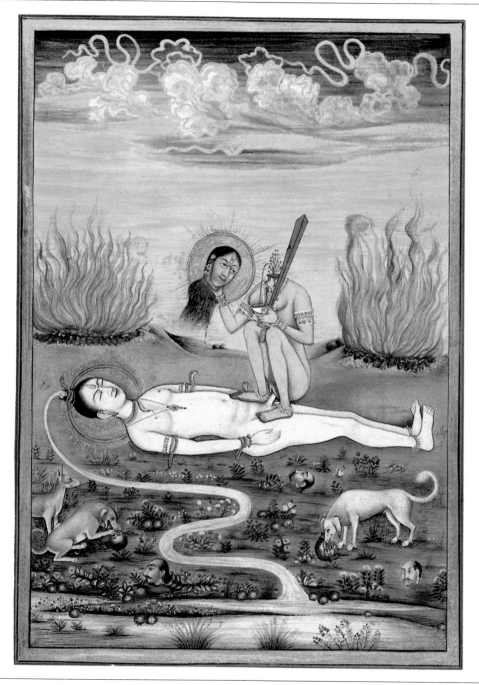

The Archetype of the Creator and Destroyer

IN the mythology of the Goddess one of the recurring themes is that of the female divinity seen as the creator and destroyer. In the mythological context, this is not seen as the war between two contrasting forces, but rather as the ambivalence of two polar opposites. The archetype stems directly from the physical experience of the menstrual cycle, the fundamental stage in the development of a young woman.

The menstrual cycle marks the times in the life of a woman which are perhaps the most vital and important, but also the most misunderstood. The body undergoes more or less dramatic physical changes which are accompanied by an alteration, during the cycle, of the physiological energy due to the fluctuation of the hormones. The discomfort provoked by the changes can nowadays be alleviated by the intake of various drugs, to aid women to partake effectively within an environment which has forgotten the functions of the natural body.

A week or so before the onset of the bleeding, the breasts may swell, the whole body may feel clumsy and accident prone, the head may ache, the intake of food may provoke unusual reactions, everything may seem to be out of synchronicity by comparison with the rest of the month. The body is responding in a way that is perhaps a warning that something of great importance is about to happen. When the lining of the womb is shed there may be an incredible upsurge of energy, which may express itself in an increase of sexual desire or, if it is internalized, in an increase of intuitive and medianic power.

There are two poles to women's sexuality; one is reached upon ovulation, expressed in terms of receptivity and surrender. This is the most fertile moment of the month, when conception is most likely to occur. The second apex of sexuality manifests itself before, during and after the menstrual flow and it is multi-orgasmic and non-fertile.(*)

---

* The authors of *The Wise Wound* [11] and *Female Cycles* [12] give a thorough explanation of the wave pattern within the female monthly cycle. The white, clear flow of ovulation is called "the river of life," because it is procreative and easily understood by the male psychology. The red flow of menstruation is called instead "the river of death," because its sexual power is totally initiated by the body of the woman without the end purpose of pregnancy.

Tantric image of "the river of death." For tantra, the human body is the microcosm, the theatre in which the psycho-cosmic drama is enacted. In the Yonitantra the menstrual flux is designated the "flower" – puspa. South India, 18th century, wood.

The ambivalence within a woman's cycle of purely creative and destructive-creative (creation through destruction) energy such as the ovulation and the menstrual period, has given rise to the archetype of woman as the creator and destroyer of life. The perfect incarnation of this archetypal image is Kali of the Hindu tradition. The Goddess represents both principles together. As the positive Divine-Mother, Lotus-Goddess, she brings worlds to birth, sustains them and absorbs them, in a never-ending cycle of her opening and closing. In her warrior aspect, Kali is the blood-thirsty, cruel and horrific Goddess dressed but with a necklace of severed heads that brings forth destruction and death in order to create.

The understanding of the female biological cycles is a first and fundamental step to the rediscovery of the inner universe of woman. It is of little use to feel degraded during menstruation because of a lack of understanding of the simple body mechanisms. In the past, when the early societies were matriarchal in their social and religious orientation, women used the upsurge of energy during the menstrual flow as a period of holy rituals and ceremonies. The first measure of time was "menstrual time," and from this the women developed lunar calendars and ancient astrology.[13]

Left: medianic power is easily accessible to a woman during her monthly cycle. During these days the unconscious permeates the conscious psyche more readily. Right: statuette depicting the primitive Mother Goddess. In this image, the divinity is protecting herself with crossed hands, for the power of the feminine cycle seizes the body, mind and soul of a woman, rendering her vulnerable to external influence. The primitives knew of the need for protection that woman seeks within herself.

The moon, because its cycle is identical to the female cycle, was revered as a divinity. Colleges of women patronized by the Goddess Hera, the moon Goddess, giver of female and natural laws, were able to influence conception and birth through dream control. In American Indian societies the menstruating woman was, and still is, seen as a powerful life source. The menstrual cycle links body, mind and soul in an unequaled tunnel of force. If made use of, as in the past, the heavy sleep characteristic of this time can be filled with prophetic dreams and the openness and vulnerability of the psyche can help a woman to reach deep states of meditation. This was the time when the priestesses went into trance-like states, looking deep into the waters of the holy wells in their sanctuaries, searching for the movements of existence within and without their bodies.

As the social system of patriarchy arose, menstruating women were seen as unclean, for the upsurge of energy that resulted from menstruation was not being used for the creation of new life, therefore making men suspicious of the female role at that time of the month. Because the woman was therefore bearing one child after another under male domination, she had no chance to experiment with her own internal movements in a creative way, such as through meditation, medianic power or rituals. These activities were a threat to male domination, and thus she transformed her natural powers into a self-destructive psychology.

Since the wide-spread use of birth control was established in the latter part of this century, we have witnessed the Women's Liberation Movement and women in general have begun to make their own voices heard for social change.

The energy released during the menstrual flow can also be greatly destructive and aggressive, but this may simply be because of a misunderstanding of our biology, not an incontrovertible truth which no woman can avoid. The energy can in fact be channeled for a more fulfilling and richer life. Mythology and the literature of the spirit relating to women have great lessons to teach on this subject; of the female power which must not be confused with the male power – its direct polar opposite.

The Archetype of the Lover / Seductress

LOVE and seduction permeate the mythology of the Goddess, for the fully flowered woman is an inexhaustible source of tender and magical feelings that transform the heart. The archetype of the lover stems from the alchemical reaction which happens when man and woman meet.

If we observe the bodies of a man and a woman facing one another, we quickly and naturally see that the woman's breasts opposite the man's flat chest and the man's protruding genitals opposite her pubic triangle form a unique and cosmic circle of power. Yin and yang, upper and lower, earth and sky – the whole universe is enclosed within the physical shape of man and woman. The immense pull to merge together to complete the circle is what we, very basically, experience as sexual energy. In the Tantric vision this force is elevated to the spiritual domain and when two Tantric lovers join together under the "blue blanket," they generate the primal energy of creation.

There is an ancient Eastern parable that says that God was bored and thus created woman for his company so that they could play together. The essence of their playing must be understood, as it differs from the Western view of the same. The Eastern idea of God is never that of a creator but that of a sacred player – a flute player, a dancer, a singer. The Eastern God creates woman, falls in love with her and plays in an endless game of hide and seek. She becomes a cow so he trans-

forms himself into a bull. Every time the woman hides in a new form she creates a new existence and God blesses it by finding her. In Western theogony, God creates a man and then out of one of the man's ribs he creates woman for the pleasure of the man. It seems then that according to the Western story, woman stands in a secondary position as a surrogate creation. Convenient to the patriarchal view, the beauty and sacredness of her existence does not possess the touch of God!

The Eastern parable follows the psychology of the relationship between man and woman. The art of seduction is to entice the male into the game and he will court and pursue the woman until she instinctively knows that the time has come to be together. The archetype of the lover and of the seductress stems from this root, the eternal dance of man chasing woman and the longing for the ultimate embrace.

Woman's orgasmic capacities are greater than man's. Out of fear of not being able to fulfill her, man has repressed woman's sexuality – women have lived and died without knowing that they have the capacity to experience orgasm. Without the full understanding of sexuality it is impossible to understand spirituality. In today's world, where sex is still to a great extent considered taboo, such a statement may even sound blasphemous. We ignore what spirituality is and we have almost no real knowledge of sex related to it.

Caparisoned bull, North India, Nathadwara, c. 1860. A well-known Indian parable sees God joyfully playing the game of hide and seek. When woman becomes a cow, the God transforms himself into a bull. Every time the woman hides in a new form she creates a new existence and God blesses it by finding her.

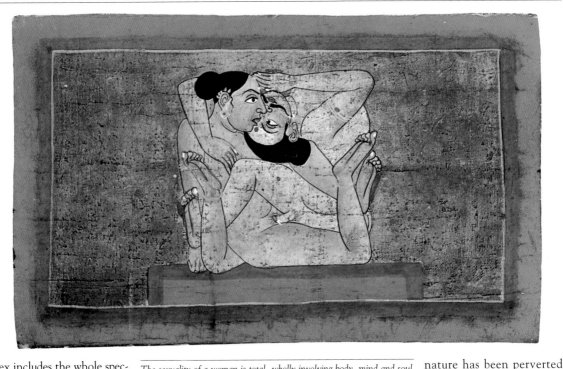

Sex includes the whole spectrum of human emotion and experience; it is fun, it is play, it is love, it is learning, it is prayer, it is meditation, it is spiritual – it is the only

The sexuality of a woman is total, wholly involving body, mind and soul in love-making. In the Tantric vision her totality is sacred. Right: "Sidonia von Bork" by Sir Edward Burne-Jones. Sidonia von Bork was a high-born but cruel sorceress, whose fatal beauty caused men to fall in love with her. Here, Sidonia is shown plotting her next crime at the court of the Dowager Dhess of Wolgast. The game of power that a woman may play in love may be very subtle, but nevertheless cruel.

nature has been perverted and misunderstood even by herself. The woman in the world is still seeking her own identity and so is the man. Her discomfort in life causes

thing in our lives that is multidimensional in its range. A woman can understand this concept because her way of loving is self-centered, it comes from her inner core. Her sexuality is total, wholly involving mind, body and soul in love-making and love relationships, whereas a man is very often left behind in his sexuality, at a point which might be compared with that of the adolescent youth.

If a religious attitude returns to the earth, then woman will regain her respect. The way of a woman is the understanding of herself and of the instinctual ways of the world, this is also the true meaning of religion. Because woman has been crippled, paralyzed, tortured, her

a disruption in the generations. Her children will not understand her psychology because she herself does not know who she is, and so the problem goes on and on.

Much depends on the freedom of a woman to find out and experience the full extent of her existence. If she is a slave, psychologically she will seek to make the man a slave too, however subtle her game may be. Perhaps she will be afraid to hit the man directly for his foolishness and she will hit herself instead, thus hen-pecking even the best of men. Only by totally freeing herself can she give freedom to others and transform it in the way of the world.

The Archetype of the Mother

THE mother archetype is perhaps the most complex and rich in the mythology of the Goddess, for it encompasses the experience of pregnancy, but more important still, it encloses the experience of birth, shared by all human beings. As we have only recently discovered, the baby within the womb is not unconscious, but is wholly aware of its feelings and surroundings. Experiments have been conducted on the memory of intra-uterine life, now proven to be carried in the collective unconscious and to emerge in dreams, hypnosis, meditation and in moments of ordinary life. There exists a deep longing in each one of us to return to the blissful existence within the womb. The mother archetype is also an important reflection of the woman's need to provide in her relationships the shelter and protection she provides for the unborn baby. When this need is fulfilled the woman feels a deep, inner satisfaction, as if she had achieved the completion of her self. It is very important to understand all the subtle nuances of this archetype, where it stems from in our psychology and physiology and how it works in our everyday lives, for it is one of the most important issues in a woman's life.

Pregnancy and birth are peak periods of life. The child experiences a dramatic transfer from the timeless, dark and reassuring life in the womb to the world of individuality and light. The terror that seizes the baby upon impact with the world outside, air filling its lungs and the sense of suffocation derived from the adjustment to the new, alien environment, is relived by the adult in any situation of great and abrupt inner change. This moment is so psychologically significant that it is amongst the most prominent features of the imagery of mythology. Not only the passage from the cosseted, womb-like environment to the world of light, but also rites of passage from life to the unknown, mystery world beyond death, have been symbolically represented the world over since prehistory.

The womb is the central psychological feature of the mythology of passage and transformation. The waters that enclose and nourish the life of the embryo in its earliest stages of growth, are symbolically represented by the motif of the circle. Goddesses, sirens, mermaids, water fairies and ladies of the lake that often appear in mythology as the guardians of wells, water courses and youth-renewing cauldrons, may represent the life-giving as well as the life-threatening aspect of water.

Within the womb, the child is unaware of the passing of time. In mythology we have images representing eternity as a retreat to the womb. There is a certain aspect to human love that transforms the man into a child and the woman into a mother, regardless of their age. The sexual impulse of penetration may take on a gentler, deeper urge to return to the darkness of the womb.

Right: Image of the Mother Goddess with symbol of reception and overflow (the horn). This symbol has remained alive from prehistory to our own day – traditionally, the wedding cake is shaped like a cornucopia, symbol of plenty. Bas relief, Laussel, Musée D'Aquitaine, Bordeaux, France.

The fear of darkness experienced by children is said to be an unconscious fear of returning to the womb, thus losing the recently acquired consciousness which may be re-absorbed in the dark, but which is strengthened by the light.

A week-old baby will wriggle its head as if trying to come out from a very narrow, spiral-like passage. The infant is re-living the moment of birth and the symbol of the spiral and of the narrow passage stays imprinted in our psyches throughout our lives. The spiral, for instance, appears spontaneously in certain stages of meditation or just before losing consciousness under the effect of ether.

We find the images of both the labyrinth and the spiral as symbols carved on many early monuments created by man. The entrances to the dark and silent Royal Irish Burial site at New Grange, probably the earliest monument erected by man, carry both symbols, for example. They have also been found in the Paleolithic caves of Southern France and Northern Spain, which strongly indicates that such sites were not only abodes, but also, and perhaps only, sanctuaries for hunting magic and the mysteries of transformation acted out as rites of passage from puberty to adulthood. The cave recesses are so deeply embedded within the bowels of the mountain, that the chambers of magic are without any worldly context and the darkness is a physical presence. The presence of such symbols on discovered sites suggests that a constellation of symbols denoting the dissolution of consciousness in the darkness of non-being must have been employed from the earliest dates as analogies of the rites of passage to the entrance in the womb of a child-spirit for birth.[14]

It is clear that the idea of birth, death and re-birth through ritual is an extremely ancient one in the history of our culture. The concept of the earth as both the bearing and nourishing mother was fundamental within the mythological and religious context of hunting societies and planters. Through the timeless archetypes of the hunters, depicted upon the walls of their caverns, one discovers that the flocks of animal life on earth were mere temporal manifestations of the Earth Mother for the nourishment of man. For the planters, the grain was sown in the mother's body, the ploughing of the earth was the insemination and the growing of the crops the birth.

The idea of the earth as mother and of death and burial as a re-entry into her womb, seems to have been the key to some of the most ancient necropolis mysteries. In the grave burials of Homo Neanderthalensis, an ancient predecessor of Homo Sapiens Sapiens, skeletons have been found in an East-West axis (like the path of the sun, the East representing the birth and the West representing the death), in a fetus-like position, as within the womb, waiting to be born again on this same earth.[15]

Above: Religious images of the ritual of life, death and re-birth of the Egyptian God Osiris. Below: Isis suckling Horus.

The relationship between the suckling baby and the mother is one of particular symbiosis. For the outer world they may appear to be two individuals, but as far as the baby is concerned, who at this stage does not differentiate between subject and object, he or she is one with the mother. "The baby's world is a continuum of consciousness, at once physical and psychic."[16] Affection, feelings, needs and satisfaction have only one focus for the early infant. The mother, for her part, almost anticipates the requirements of her baby, a deep, indescribable union linking the two.

This relationship grows steadily with the passing of the months, but it never diminishes in its importance for the psychic development of the child. It is no accident that Baudrillard has observed that "...the classic children's drawings of their mother's house, with its doors and windows, symbolizes simultaneously themselves – the human face – and the mother's body."[17]

However caring the mother may be, she cannot anticipate everything. There are moments when the universe of the baby does not respond to its needs, whereupon the first shock of separation and danger – the birth trauma – is more or less forcefully reactivated. When the mother-image begins to assume its contours in the psyche of the infant, it is of an all-embracing beatitude, but it is also associated with images of terrible danger and fear of separation. In mythology we therefore find both the sweet ambrosia of the Madonna

Below: The Owl-Goddess. The prehistoric Mother Goddess was to be depicted as a woman with the head of a bird, symbol of regeneration. The bird image was used for the flight of the soul out of the body after death and its return for reincarnation within another body. Right: The Owl-Goddess by Bosch. Even in symbolism used by painters in later historical periods, the owl remains as a powerful metaphor for inner wisdom and the regenerative powers of the feminine principle.

as well as the deathly claws of the ogress. The Judeo-Christian ideas of heaven and hell may well be a representation of the baby's universe torn apart between opposing forces of the one and only.

The archetype of the mother is a fundamental mechanism of our psyche and it appears under an almost infinite variety of aspects in the mythologies of the world. It contains both positive and negative characteristics of the same principle, as, for instance, in the mythological representation of the Norms, the Scandinavian trinity of fates: Urth (Earth), Verthandi and Skuld Urth were Mother Earth and they represented fate and the World of Creation. They lived in a cave at the source of the Fountain of Life, Urdarbrunnr, the cosmic womb.

A few examples of the mother archetype found in mythology may include as a priority the direct relationship of a hero or mythological "persona" with a mother, grand-mother, stepmother and any other woman with whom the relationship exists. Then there are mothers in what is termed the figurative sense – the Goddess, the Mother of God, the Virgin and Sophia. The mother may appear as a maiden as in the myth of Demeter and Kore, or as the beloved. The mother in the figurative sense may appear as a symbol for our longing for redemption, for example, as the Kingdom of God and Paradise, as well as in localities that inspire awe and devotion such as the Church, the country, heaven, earth, water, woods, the sea, the moon and the underworld. A ploughed field or anything standing for fertility, objects or places symbolizing the vessel such as a cave, a rock, a wood, a baptismal font or the vessel itself; all these may contain the characteristics of the mother archetype. The magic circle and the Eastern mandala remind one of the mother for the protection that they provide. The qualities inspired by the mother archetype within the individual are maternal feelings, such as the magic authority of the female, wisdom and spiritual exaltation that transcends reason, all that cherishes, sustains, grows and fosters fertility. [18]

The mother archetype finds its roots directly in the physiological experience of birth and relationship with the mother shared by all humanity. This experience is thus represented in mythological tales with their corollary of symbols in an extrapolation from the body to the soul.

The Archetype of the Priestess and Wise Woman

IN the mythology of the Goddess we find many wise women who, in their stories, help heroes and heroines to solve the riddles of existence and provide good counsel for important questions. The threshold into maturity from the sexually active years is marked by the menopause. At this time an alchemical reaction takes place within the body which is experienced psychologically as an upheaval leading into maturity and wisdom. After having lived through all the stages of physical and psychological development, a woman is finally ready to be herself, unveiled and open to the mysteries of life. This is where the archetype of the priestess and wise woman stems from, because, far from having "arrived", the woman at menopause faces yet another adventure in the seeking of her inner self. Like the perpetual motion of the waves in the sea, the movements of consciousness never meet a final threshold. Only the realization of the worldly self can lead into the understanding of the perpetual motion in the psyche. Wisdom is the knowledge that there is no end to the human search and that it is one with its goal. The archetype of the priestess and the wise woman reveals to us the intuitive wisdom which accompanies a woman throughout her life, but is most trusted and functions as the focus of energies only in the latter part of life.

Shaman dancing with spirits, miniature from the Fatik Album *of Ustat Mehmed Siyal Kalem, Turkey, c. 15th century. The shamans of contemporary hunting tribes dress with skirts, paint breasts on their chests and wear masks, before beginning a ritual. Coming in contact with the female principle enables them to enter the trance-state in which they transcend the physical laws of the body and are able to "visit" the realms of the unknown.*

Menopause is the end of the menstrual cycle, when woman enjoys perhaps her maximum freedom, independence and authority after the child-bearing years. In Native American, Hindu and African cultures the middle-aged woman is respected and often her wise advice is sought for matters of importance. The wisdom we are referring to here is instinctual in regard to things as they are and as they have always been, the innate, inherent capacity to follow the nature of things both in their present form and in their development in relation to one another.

Intuitive wisdom as described above was called Divine Sophia, from the Greek word *sophos* meaning wisdom. Sophia was the personification of wisdom, the

"The valley spirit never dies.
It is the woman, primal mother.
Her gateway is the root of heaven and earth.
It is like a veil barely seen.
Use it. It will never fail."
(Lao Tsu, Tao Te Ching)[19]

highest incarnation of the feminine principle. The experiences of motherhood, of the ambivalence of creation and destruction during the cycle and of the culminating wisdom that comes from age, are very much intermingled within the arch of a lifetime, with different psychological traits overlapping each other at any one given moment. It is true that a woman can display these and many more characteristics at one time, no matter what her age, in a kaleidoscope of psychological resourcefulness.

Above: Emile Fabry, Dream, the poet and the chimera, 1916. Right: Mythological Valkyria, the northern counterpart of the funerary vulture-priestess of Egypt.

In mythology we can see that the same richness is embodied within the *corpus* of one Goddess, in Isis, for instance, represented in ancient Egyptian mythology, the Mother of All, the nurturer. She also represented the creator and the destroyer, the theogony of Egyptian Gods and the hierarchy of Pharaohs stemming from her and owing their power to her. Isis was also called Maat, the ancient wisdom – one in all and all in one. It is only later on in the history of religions that we find one Goddess representing one archetypal characteristic, the power and richness diluted with the ages. As far back as we are now able to trace, the original Goddesses represented many principles, often as opposing as night and day and as unreasonable as woman herself.

The phases of the moon are to be compared to the three ages of woman: the new moon representing the young virgin, the full moon representing woman in her full sexual potential and the waning moon representing the wisdom of old age. The relationship between a strong Goddess and the moon is therefore interchangeable and often one Goddess may represent all three aspects of womanhood. Diana-Artemis, Goddess of the Witches (*), was the Great Goddess of the legendary Amazons. These were female warriors, wise in healing and midwifery, from ancient Thrace, Macedonia, North and West Africa and Libya. Diana in this respect was the Queen of Heaven, the pure Huntress of the Moon and Protectress of wild animals. Her followers were young women and no man was allowed to enter her temple. Diana in her second aspect was Asiatic Artemis, the orgiastic and many-breasted Mother of All. A temple of Artemis was built at Ephesus by the Amazons and it was considered one of the marvels of the ancient world. In her third form she was Hecate, Dark Goddess of the Night Sky, giver of plagues and sudden death. Hecate was worshipped at midnight, at the crossroads. The cult of Diana was observed in the Bronze Age centers throughout the Mediterranean. The original wise

woman was a warrior, a midwife, healer, leader of her tribe, strongly sexual and independent. The nature of the Goddess was overwhelming in her force of natural magic and primal wilderness. Early cultural societies were structured to accommodate a council of older women, meeting at night in the moonlight after the day's work was done, to discuss issues involving life and death, the primary domains of woman.[20]

The experience of death pertains also to the archetype of the priestess and wise woman, for true wisdom is the awareness that life and death walk together at the side of the path of life.

Death is perhaps a great misunderstanding. The archetype of the priestess and wise woman reveals through myth the proper context of death within ordinary life and it may help older women, and indeed all women, to understand and accept this passage as the beginning and end of the life cycle.

The mystery of death, one of the greatest fears of life, forms not the end of life within most forms of mythology, but very much the beginning of the new life to come. We can speculate that life is a pilgrimage towards death, from the first day we are born, since, at the moment of death, everything comes to a peak – summoned up in one instant. The greatest calamity is the misunderstanding of death, when death is regarded as taboo and everyone facing their own or their loved one's death is utterly alone and unable to comprehend the phenomenon. The wisdom of ancient times, when man lived in a natural environment, when life and death were seen every day as part of the way of existence, taught that the journey of

* The word "witch" derives from the root "wicca," meaning "wise woman." The wise women were midwives and healers, with a wide knowledge of the medicinal properties of plants and herbs. They were the early doctors. Only at the onset of patriarchy was the word "witch" given the negative connotations that still linger today.

man and his goal was one. The experience of death, of the renewal of life through death, is perhaps the most profound of all human experiences and thereby heavily permeates mythology.

Leo Frobenius pointed out in his work, *Monumenta Africana*, that two contrasting attitudes towards death can be traced amongst the primitive peoples of the world.[21] Among the hunting tribes, whose lifestyle is based on the art of killing for survival, who live in a world of animals that kill and are killed, and hardly know the organic experience of a natural death, all death is a consequence of violence and is generally ascribed to magic. Magic is employed both to defend against death and to deliver death to others, and the dead themselves are regarded as dangerous spirits, resenting their dispatch to the other world and seeking revenge among the living. Fear and magic are at the base of this attitude toward death.

For the planting folk of the fertile steppes, on the other hand, death is a natural phase of life, comparable to the moment of the planting of the seed, towards rebirth. Frobenius calls the attitude of the hunters "magical," and that of the planters "mystical." He observes that the plane of reference for the first is physical, while for the latter it represents a profound sense of communion with existence. Two contrasting attitudes towards death have fashioned two contrasting worlds of myth: one deriving from the impact of life and death in the animal sphere, the other from the model of life, death and rebirth in the plant. In the first instance the beast is consumed, the flesh eaten as part of a ritual, the skin and bones used for ornaments and clothing. The attitude of the planters, by contrast, can be seen as the Eastern non-violent approach to life, where death is an altering phase in the temporal manifestation of something which is mystical and runs its thread in existence.

"The River of Life" by William Blake, pen and water-color, c.1805.

The Archetype of the Muse

THE last archetype pertaining to the mythology and symbols of the feminine and to appear under the personification of Goddesses and other female mythological figures, is that of the woman seen as inspirer or Muse. This archetype has no recognizable foundation in the female physiology, unlike the five described so far, but nevertheless it exists in the collective unconscious of both men and women. Carl Gustav Jung, the eminent Swiss psychologist, interpreted the figure of the Muse as the manifestation of the unconscious female qualities in a man's psyche, which he termed the *anima*. The female tendencies that exist within the male psyche find their expression in moods, vague feelings, receptivity to the irrational, capacity for personal love, feelings for nature, intuitions and in the relationship to the unconscious. In mythology, the hero upon his quest seeks advice from a priestess or a sibyl who guides him by connecting him with the divine will or who causes the Gods to speak through her. The *anima* strongly influences all instinctual behavior in a man. In love relationships, for instance, a woman may feel that her partner's demands of her do not fit with what she actually wishes to be. This is the common projection of a male *anima* onto a woman. In these cases, the man's idea of womanhood may have been drawn from his psyche. Childhood memories from the mother and other comforting female presences, as well as his dreamed sexual fantasies, may shape and feed the image of the ideal woman. Men in this situation are said by women to be "mental" in their relationships.

In mythology, the *anima* is the female power which expresses the fluidity of nature's workings upon the moods of men inspiring them into seizing the irrational moment in poetry, painting, music. In a medieval text, the *anima* explains her own nature as follows :

"I am the flower of the field and the lily of the valleys. I am the mother of fair love and of fear and of knowledge and of holy hope. ... I am the mediator of the elements, making one agree with another. That which is warm I make cold and the reverse, and that which is dry I make moist and the reverse, and that which is hard I soften. ... I am the law in the priest and the word in the prophet and the counsel in the wise. I will kill and I will make to live and there is none that can deliver out of my hand." [22]

The Muse is seen in mythology as the Goddess which bridges the gap between the known and the unknown and is therefore enveloped in a veil of mystery. This archetype may work very strongly in the psyche of some women who are capable of taking the form of a man's ideal woman, becoming thus the outer manifestation of his innermost wishes. In mythology this woman is seen as a Goddess who is invariably beautiful, generous, fickle, wise, innocent and above all

Right: " Head of Girl" also known as "La Donna Scapigliata" by Leonardo da Vinci (1490), National Gallery, Parma.

Left: "The Madness of Sir
Tristram" by Sir Edward
Burne-Jones.

implacable to the mind of men.
True poetry is the bridge of passion between the sensitive man and
the highly idealized figure of the Muse,
a woman that can exist only in the trans-
parency and atemporality of human desire for
perfect love and unity.

The Muse appears as the central figure of the poetic
theme of love, death and life developed in pagan Europe
before the advent of Christianity. Originally the poet
was the leader of a totem-society of religious dancers.
His verses were danced around an altar or in a sacred
enclosure and each verse started a new turn or movement in the dance – the word "ballad" has the same
origin.[*] All the totem societies in ancient Europe were
under the dominion of the Great Goddess, the Lady of
Wild Things. Dances were seasonal and fitted into an
annual pattern from which resulted the poetic theme of
the life and death and resurrection of the Spirit of the
Year, the son and lover of the Goddess.

The archetype of the Muse incarnates more than
any other the spirit, origin and beliefs of pagan Europe
and of the Middle East, the cradle of civilization.

* From the Latin "ballare" – to dance.

The Muse is bound to love,
poetry, life and death, the annual
change of the seasons and is the
inspirer of magic and a bridge to the
unknown.

Robert Graves, in his book "The White Goddess"
which is entirely dedicated to the origins of the Muse
and poetic theme, explains the root of the word inspiration.

" 'What is inspiration?' is a question that is
continually asked. The derivation of the word
supplies two related answers. 'Inspiration' may be the
breathing-in by the poet of intoxicating fumes from an
intoxicating cauldron, …containing probably a mash of
barley, acorns, honey, bull's blood and such sacred herbs
as ivy, hellebore and laurel, or mephitic fumes from an
underground vent as at Delphi, or the fumes that rise to
the nostrils when toadstools are chewed. These fumes
induce the paranoid trance in which time is suspended,
though the mind remains active and can relate its
proleptic or analeptic apprehensions in verse.
But 'inspiration' may also refer to the inducement
of the same poetic condition by the act of listening
to the wind, the messenger of the Goddess Cardea,
in a sacred grove." [23]

The Muse is the strongest inspiring force for poetry and ritual. She appears as if in a dream or in a vision which seems to have no reality except in the consuming emptiness and longing that she leaves in the hearts of men forever after. In Spenser's *Faerie Queene*, the enchantress Phaedra is seen on a rowing-boat by the Knight Cymochiles as he wanders on the river bank. He accepts her invitation to embark with her, and they frolic together. She sings, jests, decks her head with garlands, and puts fresh flowers about her neck, to the knight's wondrous and great content. They land on an island in the "Idle lake," where she takes the "wretched thrall" to a shady dale, lulls him fast asleep with his head on her lap, and there maroons him.

The Goddess seen as Muse is the passage into oblivion and she is thus both utterly attractive and repelling. She may appear in a romantic vision as a young girl, but she is able to transform herself into a myriad of other shapes.

"Her lips were red, her looks were free,
Her locks were yellow as gold,
Her skin was white as leprosy.
The Nightmare Life-in-Death was she,
Who thicks man's blood with cold." (24)

She can become sow, mare, bitch, vixen, she-ass, serpent, owl, weasel, she-wolf, tigress, mermaid or loathsome hag.

The archetype has a base in the fear of the unknown. Due to man's extrovert psychological approach to existence, the Muse is the extrapolation in fantasy and dream of this fear. The pull toward the male-female embrace is both feared and desired and in the psychology of myth this principle is seen as feminine, as a Goddess.

The Muse does not only exist in the male unconscious, but it belongs also to the collective unconscious. Women respond to this archetype because there is a natural, inherent pull toward completion through abandon and oblivion in all existing things, almost as if life abhorred incompletion. The fact that the myth of the Muse appears in connection with the agricultural year and with life and death, and is, moreover, the ultimate aspiration and inspiration of the poet, gives further credence to its universality.

Right: "La Belle Dame Sans Merci" by Frank Cadogan Cowper. La Belle Dame is an enchantress, as Phaedra in Spenser's Faerie Queene, *who invites a knight to embark with her on a rowing-boat. She sings, jests and decks her head with garlands of flowers to the knight's great content. They land on an island in the "Idle lake," where she takes him to a shady dale, lulls him fast asleep with his head on his lap, and there maroons him.*

CHAPTER TWO

The Virgin

The Chrysalid – Artemis, the Maiden with the Silver Bow – The Archetype
of Artemis – Athene, Goddess of the Arts and Crafts –
The Archetype of Athene

The Chrysalid

HE YOUNG WOMAN who has just passed the threshold of puberty and is now facing a new life of the senses and of the psyche, can be compared to a butterfly who has begun to spread her wings on a spring day. Animated by youthful and positive energy, the young virgin sees life as a vastness of colors and shapes all of which have become available to her. Her impulse to fly is undaunted.

The archetype of the virgin represents that part of woman which is "untouched" by worldly bonds, which has remained pure and uncorrupted. It does not mean that she is literally and physically virginal. She speaks and lives only her own truth and is straightforward in her actions, following only her own instincts.

When this archetype is dominant in a woman's psyche, the characteristic that is most noticeable in her relationship with others is that she is her own master. Her capacity to search her own spirit and pin-point exactly what is best for her at any given moment, as if she possessed a magical torch of wise intuition, helps her to keep to her own track and to be unmoved by the reaction of others toward her decisions. There is in this characteristic a freedom of spirit which causes "virgin women" to undertake actions and fulfill roles which may not be the traditional ones. For example, she may not be interested in such events as motherhood or marriage. A virgin woman may decide to dedicate her life to the spiritual search for the self and she may enter an ashram or a monastery in order to practice meditation. She may also possess great courage for adventure in both her personal and career life. Women who undertake such daring pastimes as mountain climbing, piloting aircraft, hunting or sea-faring, often display the qualities of the virgin archetype.

Another strong characteristic of the virgin woman is whole-hearted behavior in everything she does. She will only take on a commitment, for instance, if she truly knows that she will be able to fulfill it totally. This she does not do simply to please or to gain praise, but as a genuine desire to move and change her relationship with others.

The virgin characteristic also contains the ability to judge personal limits fairly. A virgin woman is a formidable counselor in times of need, for her response to each situation stems from her own freedom. She is able to extricate problems from the entanglements of compromise and the fear of assertion. Her focus is on individuality, her own and that of others, and she values above all else the maintenance of the personal unbound self. A woman in distress over love affairs, for instance, may greatly benefit from friendship with a virgin woman, for she will be helped in recognizing the patterns that have led her to focus more on the lover than on herself – often the cause of marital trouble.

Artemis – the Maiden with the Silver Bow

THE beauty of a virgin woman is her untroubled enthusiasm and freshness for life. It is almost as if her heart were a pool of clear water, unattached to all that society and conventions dictate, always ready to receive, fearlessly, the gifts that existence bestows upon her. Like the blue depths of a mountain lake, she is deeply intuitive and does not hesitate in taking action once she has decided over the course of events. The virgin woman stands apart from all other women, for she has not bent her will into compromise to gain an easy life. She may find herself sometimes alone, like Artemis, the Goddess of the Hunt, who lived in the woods. The virgin woman has plenty of psychological resources and she uses her creativity as an expression of her spirit. Women painters, writers, poets and other creators display all the characteristics of the virgin archetype. The quality of the virgin gives the woman the opportunity to feel whole without a man, absolutely fulfilled by her own existence and enjoyment of life. In her relationships, she is always an individual, recognizing that the fusion with the other is not the ultimate goal in her search for the self. She gives freedom in her relationships for she greatly values this quality in her own life.

The following are some of the myths that tell of the virgin Goddesses. If we unravel their symbolism, we are able to see how the archetype may work in a woman's everyday life.

Artemis was the daughter of Zeus, the chief God of the Greek pantheon, and of Leto. When Hera, the wife of Zeus, discovered the amorous intrigue she became so jealous and enraged that she sent the serpent Python to pursue pregnant Leto and decreed that she should not be delivered in any place where the sun shone. Leto came at last to Ortygia, where she bore Artemis painlessly. As soon as little Artemis was born she helped her mother across narrow straits and there she delivered her of Apollo, after nine days of labor.

One day, while she was still a small child, her father Zeus asked her what presents she would like. Artemis answered at once: 'Pray give me eternal virginity; as many names as my brother Apollo; a bow and arrows like his; the office of bringing light; a saffron tunic with a red hem reaching to my knees; and many nymphs from the ocean as my maids of honor.' Zeus granted all this and made her guardian of the roads and harbors of thirty cities. Artemis was already patron of childbirth as her mother Leto carried her and bore her with no pain.

She asked the Cyclopes to build for her a silver bow and some arrows, in return for which they would eat the first prey she brought down.

Artemis required the same perfect chastity from her companions as she practiced herself. On one occasion, Actaeon stood leaning against a rock to watch Artemis bathing in a stream. Lest he should afterwards dare boast to his companions that she had displayed herself naked in his presence, she changed him into a stag and commanded his own pack of hounds to tear him into pieces. [25]

Left: Venus of Brassempouy, France. An early depiction of the Goddess of the Hunt. Right: "After the Bath" by Raphaelle Peale, Nelson Gallery, Atkins Museum, Kansas City, Missouri. In classical Greek mythology, the feminine bath is symbol of the renewal of purity and virginity, a sacred act undertaken by the priestesses of the Goddess.

The silver bow of Artemis represents the new moon, symbol of the Maiden or Virgin. She is the protectress of childbirth and also of death, as her killing arrows testify. Young girls of nine entered the service of Artemis as her priestesses, reminding the worshipers of the Goddess that the moon's death number is three times three (three phases of the moon). The purification bath during which Artemis is surprised by Actaeon, is the symbol of a ritual bath which was performed by her priestesses in order to maintain their purity and virginity intact.

"Brunnhilde" ("Die Goetterdammerung" final scene) by Odilon Redon. Lithograph illustration for the "Revue Wagnerienne," 1885. The clear wisdom of the Virgin has often been depicted in the form of warrior-maidens fighting a battle with the gods of chaos, for the force of the archetype illuminates the path of reason, as described in the myth of Artemis.

The Archetype of Artemis

NIVERSALLY KNOWN AS THE Goddess of the Hunt, Artemis represents the independent and free feminine spirit. When Zeus offers her presents of her own choice, she asks, without a shadow of doubt even though she is still a small child, for all those qualities and things she knows will be the fundamental instruments for the fulfillment of her own nature. This is an important passage in the myth of the Goddess Artemis, for it represents the concept that the woman in whom the virgin archetype is working possesses a clear vision concerning the course of her own life. An innate, intuitive wisdom guides her towards the right decisions, even though these may be against social conditioning. She knows, for instance, which are the best and most profitable investments. She knows how to choose the best marriage partner or what moves to undertake in her career. Seen from the outside, this quality in a virgin woman may be mistaken for a capricious nature in the sense that she may be seen by others to be one always to get her own way, regardless of opposition. But this is not the whole story, for the virgin woman is simply following her innate ability to chose the best, thus giving an exterior impression of good fortune to those less fortunate and perhaps envious of her life.

The presents that the Goddess Artemis asks of her father are symbols which, when unraveled, may be seen as the fundamental milestones in the life of a virgin woman. The gift of eternal virginity, for instance, stands for the wish to always remain "true to her own nature," uncorrupted and pure in the expression of the self. The virgin woman cannot, on any grounds, enter a relationship, whether with a lover, a friend or a working partner, in which she would have to be other than what she is. The "loss of virginity" that such a false relationship would entail would cause extreme pain and psychological disruption. She would freeze, as it were, and be totally unable to function. Her uncontaminated nature is often the mirror for the faults and corruption of others, even though this reflection may be totally unintended. In fact, the name Artemis means "water," that which reflects reality back to the onlooker.

Artemis asks Zeus for bow and arrows. The bow, as we have seen previously, stands as a metaphor for the New Moon, symbol of the Maiden. The shooting of the arrows can be seen as a symbol for the expression of the self. The arrows may represent wishes, actions, decisions. The bow is, however, made from the moon, which means that the origin of her expression is moonlike, intuitive, of a hidden, mysterious nature. The virgin woman who finds affinities with Artemis may not be able logically to explain why she is doing what she is doing. She knows only that it is right. And not until she has fulfilled her enterprise can she decipher her internal movements, for they remain hidden until they are fully and finally expressed.

Gustav Klimt. *"... the third gift, the office of bringing light as a symbol for helping others in their path."*

The third gift is the office of bringing light, a symbol for helping others in their own paths. It is almost a duty for the virgin woman to share with others her gift of clear sight, helping to distinguish important issues from the intricacies of events and feelings. Artemis was also known as the Goddess of the Hunt; in Rome she was called Diana and was believed to hunt in the moonlight with her pack of hounds. The Artemis woman is able to see clearly through the dark woods of human affairs, guided by the light of the moon – by her intuition. Like a hunter, she follows the tracks of animals, aware of every scent, every movement in the night shadows of the forest. The hunter and hunted are one in the moment of death; before striking death with her arrow, Artemis is in deep communion with the prey and has an almost religious understanding of death and change of destiny. When the Artemis woman decides to change the course of events either in her own life or in the life of a friend who has sought her counsel, she is fully aware of the implications that such a change would entail without, however, hesitating to make a clear cut with the past.

The Goddess Artemis is also patroness of childbirth. The natural events in a woman's life such as pregnancy, childbirth and sexuality should be lived "painlessly" as in the myth, for they are part of her true nature and the Artemis woman reveres this highly. She

has unbounded energy for the propagation of this understanding and her wrath is unleashed when nature is, in her eyes, corrupted. In the myth we see this in the punishment of Actaeon, who dared look upon the divine with the arrogance of human desire. One of the most cherished values of the Artemis woman is respect for mutual relationships; when this is ignored or given ill consideration she strikes out violently, perhaps deeply upsetting a situation which was never intended to be malicious, but nevertheless interpreted as such by her in her excessive zeal. The wisdom of old age can teach the Artemis woman compassion toward the corruptibility of human nature.

In ancient Greece, the worship of the Goddess Artemis was also the worship of the Goddess's main qualities; inner focus and strength in one's own individuality. One of the rituals associated with Artemis was the observation and celebration of the movements of the Great She-Bear or Ursa Major constellation in the night sky, which was believed to be the animal incarnation of the Goddess. As it revolves around the Polar Star at its center, month after month, the constellation indicates with its tail the advent of the four seasons – pointing to the east it announces the arrival of spring, pointing to the south the arrival of summer, to the west the arrival of autumn and to the north the arrival of winter. The worship of the She-Bear Artemis encompassed thus astronomical

Athene, Goddess of the Arts and Crafts

"According to the Pelasgians, the Goddess Athene was born beside Lake Tritonis in Libya, where she was found and nurtured by the three nymphs of Libya. As a girl, she killed her playmate, Pallas, by accident while they were engaged in friendly combat with spear and shield, and in token of grief, she set Pallas's name before her own and became known as Pallas Athene.

Athene invented the flute, the trumpet, the earthenware pot, the plough, the rake, the ox-yoke, the horse-bridle, the chariot, and the ship. She first taught the science of numbers, and all women's arts, such as cooking, weaving, and spinning. Although a Goddess of war, she gets no pleasure from battle, but rather from settling disputes, and upholding the law by pacific means. She bears no arms in times of peace. Her mercy is great: when the judges' votes are equal in a criminal trial, she always gives a casting vote to liberate the accused. Yet, once engaged in battle, she never loses the day, even against Ares (the God of War) himself, being better grounded in tactics and strategy than he; and wise captains always approach her for advice." [26]

observations with religious expression and the understanding of the seasons' power over life.

The woman who wishes to cultivate the qualities of Artemis or strengthen the archetype within her, must, like the Ursa Major constellation, encompass the inner focus and strength in her own convictions at her center. If the cultivation of Artemis becomes her primary motivation she will always have a source of fulfilling "self-worth," which may guide her through the "seasons" of her life. Artemis is a strong and drastic Goddess for the cultivation of her archetype demands that a woman never corrupt her own "virginity," remaining always true to herself.

A THENE is the Goddess of Wisdom. In Roman mythology she was also known as Minerva and she was often portrayed with an owl: the hunting, and yet homely, bird of the night. According to other versions of her myth, she was born from the head of Zeus and in her deeds she came often to the aid of heroic gods and acted as their strategist for war.

Above left: The Owl-Goddess, Neser, Peru. Athene was often portrayed with an owl, the hunting, and yet homely, bird of the night. Right: The head of Athene represents wisdom, and shows the dynamic energy fields of the pineal and pituitary glands blending to form the third or spiritual eye.

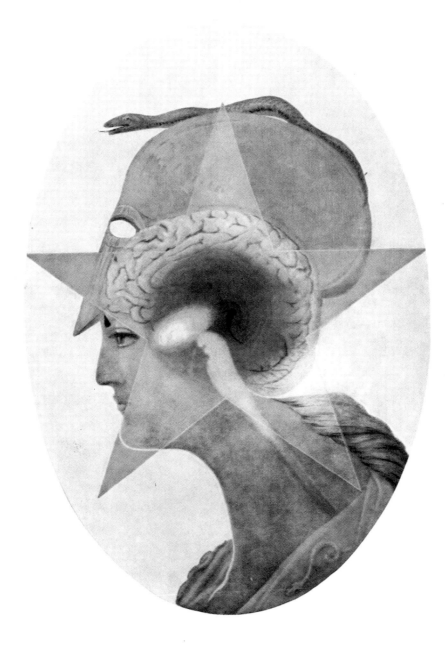

The Archetype of Athene

THE VIRGIN ARCHETYPE represented by Athene reveals feminine logic and practical acumen. In the myth, Athene invents a number of useful devices which help man to tame nature, such as the horse-bridle for use in both war and agriculture, the ship to explore unknown lands, increase trade of commodities and master both winds and waters. The plough, the rake and the ox-yoke are also her invention to facilitate and increase the results of man's work on the land. The taming of nature for good purposes is an important aspect of this archetype, for it reveals the deep understanding of both man's nature and the workings of nature itself. What is most important about this central aspect of the archetype, is that Athene is able to apply her intuition and understanding in a practical, useful way. Perhaps this is best explained by the example of Athene as a war strategist. She understands the human impulse to make war and sees it as a positive tool to conquer new lands or defeat an enemy. She is able to apply this understanding by drawing a practical war plan, as if she could see the whole situation with all its implications as one. Like the owl, Athene observes with one eye the movements, impulses, strengths, weaknesses, advantages and disadvantages of the attackers and of the attacked in the war scene. With the other eye (the owl has one eye open and the other closed) she draws from her intuitive knowledge to plan the final and decisive move. The comparison with a nocturnal bird of prey is in fact very appropriate, for in order to hunt successfully while flying, these birds need to know intimately the nature of their prey as well as their own limits and capacities and the conditions of nature during the night hunt.

Women who find affinities with the virgin archetype as expressed in the figure of Athene may well be, for instance, successful commodity brokers who are able to detect instinctively the movements in the market and act accordingly with planned time and strategy. They may also be successful career women, able to stir in the meanders of corporate policies and inner competition. The Athene woman has the gift of logical, feminine thinking, which is intuitive in its nature. She is able to maintain a clear head amidst powerful emotions and to provide practical solutions for intricate problems. The Athene woman is a fair judge, as told in the myth, and can be an excellent career adviser or business consultant, helping to provide companies with carefully worked-out business management programs.

Always flanked by heroes, powerful gods and even believed in some instances to have been born from Zeus's brow, Athene may appear as "masculine" as well as very mature in her nature. Without doubt, she possesses a moral and psychological integrity which is very different from the gifts owned by Artemis or any other Goddess. Her wisdom is practical, her tactics cold and

"Pallas Athene" by Gustav Klimt, (1898).

determined. Moreover, war is a typical male occupation. In this, Athene is a virgin Goddess for she is set apart from the other more traditional Goddesses. But her gift for strategy implies that she is aware of ethics and diplomacy, recognizing the power of the opponent and respecting it. It may therefore be that a woman with Athene's characteristics could be misunderstood by other women, for she is not felt to be "feminine" enough. She is, however, easily able to overcome this first reaction by her understanding of others.

Powerful men may often relate to and rely upon the counsel of the woman with Athene qualities. Her relationship with them is one of equality and respect, for she is at ease in the male world and its avenues are not a mystery.

unfolding of events. Athene is also master of destiny, flowing in its current. The woman with Athene qualities may be, in her later years, almost like a magician, a strategist of fate, counseling others in how to further their own projects for a deeply satisfying life.

The sign of Athene is a triangle placed on top of a reversed cross, symbol of inner direction and knowledge of one's own capabilities. Both men and women in ancient Greece worshipped Athene when they needed to strengthen the qualities represented by the Goddess. Before war or before making an important decision in political or family matters, for instance, the ancient Greeks would ascend to the temple dedicated to the Goddess and spend some time in quiet meditation. The ritual to invoke the powers and favor of the

Athene invented also the flute, the trumpet and the earthenware pot, and was teacher of all women's arts, including cooking, weaving and spinning. This is a symbol for her deeply feminine nature, the meditative peace and the appreciation of matter and time. The production of sound from a wooden instrument such as the flute, or the mixing and preparing of foods are examples of an alchemical transformation, which she understands and is master of. Weaving and spinning are metaphors for the weaving of time, the

Goddess so that she might, with her divine strength, induce clarity and inner direction was a private one, personal to each who worshipped before her, for Athene aided the force of clear wisdom in the individual to become manifest.

This archetype becomes active in a woman when she calls for the qualities represented by Athene to become manifest within her. Education, any kind of discipline applied to abstract subjects such as mathematics, scientific research and analysis, or applied to

inner disciplines such as yoga, tai chi, and thoroughness in work, are good channels to invoke the power of the Goddess, for they strengthen in the individual, objectivity, skill and mental focus. Athene influences a woman in achieving personal fulfillment through a career; when she takes examinations or prepares with thoroughness and skill for a degree or some aspect of her work which will increase her capabilities, in these cases the archetype is at work.

Left: Athene was teacher of all women's arts, including cooking, weaving and spinning. She was also the inventor of the flute. Above: Etruscan wall painting depicting an aristocratic lady.

CHAPTER THREE

Creator and Destroyer

The Polarities of Oneness – Kali, the Incarnation of the Feminine Force –
The Archetype of Kali – Circe, The Sorceress – The Archetype of Circe –
Medea, the Murderess – The Archetype of Medea –
The Children of The Sea

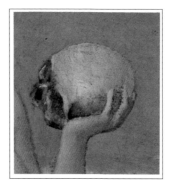

The Polarities of Oneness

HROUGHOUT THE ANCIENT world the Goddess was worshipped for her dual creative and destructive power. She was symbol of all the opposites in life, encapsulating in her figure the respect that the ancients had for a life in which good or bad events, divine and evil, combined themselves in completion. The Goddesses of the ancient world were thus creative and destructive, good-natured and malignant, brought about birth and death, were saintly and sexual. These attributes were not seen as opposites, but rather as polarities of "oneness"; existence could not be conceived with one and not the other. The richness of the mythology of the Goddess stems from the merging together of all the forces that govern our universe into one persona.

The archetype of the polarity of creation and destruction finds its roots in the monthly cycle of woman. Two peak periods mark the monthly event: ovulation and menstruation. During ovulation, woman is at her most fertile. A white flow, which has been called by the ancients the "river of life," marks the onset of ovulation. The hormonal change produces an upsurge of sexuality which is expressed in terms of tender love. A woman may feel she wants protection from her partner and a gentle, caring love-making. The other peak arrives with menstruation. The shedding of the lining of the womb produces a flow of blood, which has been called by the ancients

"the river of death," as it is a dispersion of that which has not been impregnated. During these days there occurs another increase in sexual energy, which is most often not expressed as such, but becomes a violent mood which drives the woman to more or less destructive tendencies. It is as if the body had suddenly become a pressure chamber. In many ways menstruation is a more dramatic and powerful event than ovulation and is experienced by women in more traumatic terms. If during ovulation one may seek the care of the partner, during menstruation the opposite is achieved through troublesome moods and emotional outbursts. Centuries of repression and exclusion from social activities during the days of menstruation have driven women to a misunderstanding of the "destructive" mood. Creation can happen also through destruction of the old, and it is, in fact, a more permanent and constructive action.

From the earliest times the belief that there is a connection between woman and the moon has been held in almost all parts of the world. The woman's power to bear children, for instance, was regarded as a mystery gift of the moon. The female cycle, which is the same as the cycle of the moon, must have seemed to primitive man the natural result of a mysterious bond between woman and the moon. Some North American Indians regard the moon as a woman and when it is waning they believe she is having her "sickness," which is the term they use to indicate menstrua-

tion. In other languages the terms for menstruation and moon are closely related. In French, for instance, the menstrual period is called *le moment de la lune*.[27] Thus the primary symbol for the creator and the destroyer is the moon. In its different phases it represents the different ebbs and flows of a woman's monthly cycle. Sometimes the moon also stands for the Goddess.

During menstrual period women, almost universally, were put under severe restrictions and banned from social activities. Women were considered taboo and many tribes believed that anything a menstruating woman touched would lose its "power." Thus, special huts were devised into which women could retire during their "sickness." Unfortunately however, the extent of the taboo was far wider-reaching than just the mere objects that could not be touched in a woman's surrounding. For instance, among primitive people today, when a woman is under the menstrual taboo she may not come near nor encounter any man. Her shadow is polluting, so she must keep well away from all other members of the tribe. Her "uncleanliness" is considered to be worse than an actual bacterial infection, and everything touched by her is immediately contaminated. In some tribes, the woman is not allowed by this same moral attitude to touch even her own body. A stick is given to her for scratching her head. If the woman does not obey the laws that keep her at a safe distance from the rest of the tribe, and she happens inadvertently to touch something, it is believed that famine, sickness and death will strike the members of the tribe. It is still believed today in the less advanced regions of Europe, such as in certain parts of Italy, Spain, Portugal and Greece that it is dangerous to bathe or take too many showers during menstruation, that a girl or woman should not swim nor do gymnastics, that it is dangerous for her to wash her hair because the heat of the belly would go to warm up the head and thus cause disruptions in the menstrual flow, which will thereby last longer. They believe also that it is inappropriate to wear bright colors and women should chose darker shades, as if in mourning. Making love during menstruation is regarded by many women as "not right."

The menstrual taboo is perhaps one of the oldest of mankind's taboos. But blood is also as much part of life in both primitive and contemporary societies as death and birth, so that the root cause of the menstrual "curse" lies deep in the recesses of the human psyche.

One of the most common beliefs that we find lurking in primitive social structures is associated with woman's impurity during menstruation and this is in turn associated with her possession by evils spirits. The primitive methods for exorcising possession include fasting, purging or fumigation with smoke, all such techniques being practiced in the women's hut.

But what is this evil that enters woman once a month? From the physiological viewpoint we must return to the upsurge of sexual energy in order to find an answer. The increase of sexuality during menstruation does not have as its end product the creation of a baby, the natural result of love-making during ovulation. There is perhaps then an upsurge in energy for the purpose of physical pleasure. There also exists medical evidence to the effect that a woman feels a deeper and more orgasmic pleasure during menstruation than at any other time in the month. This is perhaps where the knot lies, for the orgasmic capacity of woman is stronger than that of man only in so far as it touches the whole of her body and her psyche giving a more lasting effect. In fact, it was a popular belief that a woman during menstruation was able to "unman"

a man. Woman's heightened sexual capacity must have represented a threat to man, for he either gave in to it and became "sex-drunk," and thus unable to perform his social duties, or he repressed his urge by repressing woman. But this "destructive" effect of woman could sometimes be used to cure evil. A popular practice to disinfest a field from caterpillars was to have a menstruating girl run totally naked around it three times. It was firmly believed that the caterpillars would die by the next morning and the harvest would be saved. The destructive power was used to drive away evil, and this rural practice hides in its simplicity a deeper truth.

Today we are aware that sexuality is but one of the many expressions of physiological energy. The same upsurge can be used as a time of enrichment. In primitive communities a period of seclusion was prescribed during the "illness" and it may be that a need for solitude still exists in the modern woman, even though it may not be recognized as a psychological necessity. The nature of woman is cyclic, fluctuating in ebbs and flows during the month. Restlessness, inertia and a general sense of disharmony are the physical and psychological signs that this natural state is being undermined. Our tendency in modern society is to go about our business without regard for the inner movements of the body so that we rarely get the chance to observe the true changes that take place during menstruation. Perhaps a period of introversion and seclusion is valuable to the modern woman, so that she may regain for herself the wisdom of the ancients.

Ancient temple techniques for women during menstruation included meditation, gentle forms of hypnosis, massage and aromatherapy which soothed the body and calmed the spirit; today such methods are available once again. The seclusion and "turning in" of such methods can produce as much creative power as the conception of a child, and women of today have granted themselves a choice in this matter after centuries of repression and encapsulation in the forced role of the baby factory.

The mythology of the creator and destroyer contains powerful symbols for the ambivalence of woman's cyclic nature. The movements of the unconscious that seize her during the hormonal changes in the monthly cycle have been transported to the higher plane of myth and fantasy, in which Goddesses are able to create and destroy worlds and entities at will.

Right: "Melancolia" by Albrecht Dürer, Gabinetto delle Stampe, Galleria degli Uffizi, Florence. Restlessness, inertia and a sense of disharmony can affect the moods of a woman.

Kali – The Incarnation of the Feminine Force

"Kali manifested herself for the annihilation of demonic male power in order to restore peace and equilibrium. For a long time asuric (demonic) forces had been dominating and oppressing the world.
Even the powerful gods were helpless and suffered defeat at their hands. They fled pell-mell in utter humiliation, a state hardly fit for the divine.
Finally they prayed in desperation to the Daughter of the Himalayas to save gods and men alike. The gods sent forth their energies as a steam of fire, and from these energies emerged the Great Goddess Durga.
In the great battle to destroy the most arrogant and truculent man-beasts, the Goddess Kali sprang forth from the brow of Durga to join in the fierce fighting." [28]

KALI is perhaps one of the most intoxicating personifications of primal energy expressed in the form of a Goddess. This Hindu myth survives to this day and Kali is worshipped as one of the main divinities of India. She represents an overwhelming intensity and a mighty strength. When she sprang forth from the brow of Durga, the skies were filled with a mighty roar.

Leonie Caldecott in her book *"The Dance of the Woman Warrior"* gives us a valuable glimpse of the function of Kali according to the myth:

"What is there in the story (of Durga) for us? Well, to start with, the fact that the gods could not change the situation themselves, and they had to create a Goddess, not another god, to do it for them. In a deadlock situation, the woman is the only moving element. Another thing worth noting is that the dualism gods/anti-gods, good/evil, has a lot to do with the deadlock, a fact which is far from irrelevant to the actual cold wars with which military powers play in the world today. That dualism also makes a point of keeping women in their place, making the female condition the undesirable half of the dualistic equation. The only way that Durga can alter the consequences of this division is by employing an adaptability not normally under the dualistic regime...."

Durga slaying the demon Mahishasura.

The Goddess Kali succeeds in defeating the demons with her primary power. The mighty roar could be said to be the physical manifestation that this powerful archetype has upon the human psyche when it is met. She is thus the representation of the dualism that saves life from becoming a torment inflicted by demons. The splitting off of reality into moral judgments of good/evil, mine/yours, pure/corrupt, and so on, is the source of all evil on earth. Kali wipes everything away restoring existence to its natural way so that the gods may come back bringing an undivided view of life.

This awe-inspiring Goddess is the personification of the good and terrible mother, of the creator and destroyer in all its grandiose form of life, love, death and destruction. She is traditionally portrayed as the Black Mother, squatting over her dead consort Shiva, eating his entrails while her yoni is sexually devouring his lingam. Worshipers of Kali must accept death as part of her Curse for she represents both sides of the coin of existence. The Goddess was the personification of the eternal living flux, from which all things rose and then disappeared. She was the material cause of all change, manifestation and destruction.

Blood was a strong part of Kali's worship as a traveler to her temple in India reported:

"The temple simply serves as a slaughterhouse, for those performing the sacrifice retain their animals, leaving only the head in the temple as a symbolic gift, while the blood flows to the Goddess. For to the Goddess is due the life blood of all creatures – since it is she who has bestowed it – and that is why the beast must be slaughtered in her temple. That is why slaughterhouse and temple are one.

This rite is performed amid gruesome filth. In the mud compounded of blood and earth, the heads of the animals are heaped up like trophies before the statue of the Goddess, while those sacrificing return home for a family banquet of the bodies of their animals. The Goddess desires only the blood of the offerings, hence beheading is the form of sacrifice, since the blood drains quickly from the beheaded beasts .... The head signifies the whole, the total sacrifice.*"* [30]

Though the Goddess is one, according to the capability and desire of the worshiper, she is conceived of in innumerable forms. She is the source of all energies and the feminine divinities emanating from her are represented in descending order of importance. Some are fractions of her power, some are partial emanations, and all women are considered to be "fractions of fractions" of her power. When all the different manifestations come together, they represent the full power of the archetype.

India is perhaps the only country to have retained the image of the Goddess in her primal manifestation. Her myth is often misunderstood, especially so by Western anthropologists, who saw in her just the thirst for blood and destruction of the perverted and unsophisticated barbarians. If we see the world and its varying customs as a representation of our collective unconscious, then the myth and worship of Kali is that part of the memory, deep and distant, which reflects the primary forces of nature. These forces form the cycles of woman, her inner movements mirroring the powerful flow of existence.

The Archetype of Kali

T HE ARCHETYPE REPRESENTED by Kali is possibly the most powerful and crude in the mythology of the Feminine. It is perhaps difficult to understand, in our age of sophisticated social relationships and morally filtered expressions of feelings, how this archetype may influence the life of an ordinary, modern woman.

The author had a direct experience of the archetype working in the psyche of a young woman when visiting a female penitentiary in Southern India. In a small courtyard, set apart from the rest of the building and fenced around by tall walls, there was a young woman of approximately twenty-five years of age. She was kneeling down and the upper part of her body swayed rhythmically to her loud invocation of the Goddess Kali. The guide to the penitentiary told us her sad story. Married, with three small children, she had become infatuated with the blood-thirsty Goddess Kali and began praying to the divinity in order to gain psychic power. One night, she had killed her husband and cut to pieces her three children with an ordinary kitchen knife.

This is a negative, cruel example of the influence of such a powerful archetype upon an ordinary girl, one among many others in the vast population of the Asian sub-continent.

The creator and destroyer archetype as manifested in the Goddess Kali does not often arise in a woman's psyche, especially in today's world. Its effects are the expression of raw, animal-like emotions which, even though always denied, nevertheless exist in the stored memory of a lifetime. There has been a lot of experimentation in modern psychology over the last one and a half decades with what is termed experiential therapy. This kind of treatment, for which there are a variety of methods, has the effect of unlocking powerful events from a repressed, unconscious psyche. These experiences may have affected the individual in a traumatic way and may be in the order of rape, incest, physical violence. These are still considered taboo by the social structure, and a person who has lived through such a trauma will generally find a wall of cold indifference from others. The Kali archetype may be activated when a woman enters the "therapy chambers"; a mysterious symbiosis occurs between the therapist and the patient, for the first must unlock the repressed pain with the same force with which it needs to be expressed. It may therefore be that both women, therapist and patient, are temporarily under the effect of the Kali archetype, recreating the memory of the trauma and destroying it as it is being expressed. The success of the therapy depends on the total, unbounded and unconditioned "let-go" of the patient,

"The Vampire" by Edward Munch. In popular imagination the vampire was seen as a woman, symbol of raw, animal-like emotions.

Circe – the Sorceress

THE myth of Circe is found in Homer's tale of Odysseus's wanderings for ten years in the Mediterranean Sea. On his adventurous journey, at the mercy of the winds, Ulysses reaches the enchanted island where Circe dwells.

"He (Ulysses) steered his sole remaining vessel due east and, after a long voyage, reached Aenea, the Island of Dawn, ruled over by the Goddess Circe, daughter of Helius and Perse, and thus sister to Aeetes, the baleful king of Colchis. Circe was skilled in all enchantments, but had little love for human-kind. When lots were cast to decide who should stay to guard the ships and who should reconnoiter the island, Odysseus's mate Eurylochus was chosen to go ashore with twenty-two others. He found Aenea rich in oaks and other forest trees, and at last came upon Circe's palace, built in a wide clearing towards the center of the island. Wolves and lions prowled around but, instead of attacking Eurylochus and his party, stood upright on their hind legs and caressed them. One might have taken these beasts for human beings, and so indeed they were, though thus transformed by Circe's spells.

Circe sat in her hall, singing to her loom and, when Eurylochus's party raised a halloo, stepped out with a smile and invited them to dine at her table. All entered gladly, except Eurylochus himself who, suspecting a trap, stayed behind and peered anxiously in at the windows. The Goddess set a mess of cheese, barley, honey, and wine before the hungry sailors. But it was drugged, and no sooner had they begun to eat than she struck their shoulders with her wand and transformed

who literally, cleans her soul from the mark of destiny. This is the primary meaning of the Kali archetype – the total destruction of evil in order to create a fresh and clean slate of consciousness.

The activation of the creator and destroyer archetype as represented by Kali is exceptional in its impact and results, for when it is unlocked the woman must have previously decided to cut away, kill forever, an evil shadow in her psyche. Through destruction she willingly drives herself to creation. The archetype is so powerful that its activation must always be watched over by an expert of human psychology who will guide it toward completion, without leaving the trauma unresolved to haunt the psyche of the patient.

Left: Image of blood-thirsty Kali. Right: "The Seduction of Merlin" by Sir Edward Burne-Jones. In the Celtic legend, Morgain seduced the wizard Merlin by using her sorcery.

them into hogs. Grimly then she opened the wicket of a sty, scattered a few handfuls of acorns and cornel-cherries on the miry floor, and left them there to wallow.

Eurylochus came back, weeping, and reported this misfortune to Odysseus, who seized his sword and went off, bent on rescue, though without any settled plan in his head. To his surprise he encountered the god Hermes, who greeted him politely and offered him a charm against Circe's magic : a scented white flower with a black root, called moly, which only the gods can recognize and cull. Odysseus accepted the gift gratefully and, continuing on his way, was in due course entertained by Circe. When he had eaten his drugged meal, she raised her wand and struck him on the shoulder. 'Go join your comrades in the sty' she commanded. But having surreptitiously smelt the moly flower, he remained unenchanted, and leapt up, sword in hand. Circe fell weeping at his feet. 'Spare me' she cried ' and you shall share my couch and reign in Aenea with me!' Well aware that witches have power to enervate and destroy their lovers, by secretly drawing off their blood in little bladders, Odysseus exacted a solemn oath from Circe not to plot any further mischief against him. This oath she swore by the blessed gods and, after giving him a deliciously warm bath, wine in golden cups, and a tasty supper served by a staid housekeeper, prepared to pass the night with him in a purple coverleted bed. Yet Odysseus would not respond to her amorous advances until she consented to free not only his comrades but all the other sailors enchanted by her. Once this was done, he gladly stayed in Aenea until she had borne him three sons, Agrius, Latinus and Telegonos." [31]

"The Beginning of Life" by F. Kupka. Sorcery works in a circle which brings all things to an end in order to start them anew.

Right: Circe's Circle. Circe is here seen weaving, but her apparent domesticity hides her sorcery for the thread she spins is the weaving of the destiny of men.

The island of Circe was located beyond east and west, where dawn rose. The Greeks believed the island to be off the coast of Italy, in an area known today as Monte Circeo. This small peninsula, connected to the mainland by a swampy path, is still covered with lush vegetation, just as one might imagine Circe's mythical land to be. Lions and wolves, perhaps symbols of the Goddess of Wild Beasts, live there in the myth, all so tame as to persuade us that they are bewitched humans with Circe also present – the inheritor of the Great Goddess – her magic as her divine power. That divine sorcery revolves around love-magic, in her wish to arouse love through power. She encircles her victims within her dwelling and offers them drugged food. The name Circe stands for "circle" – symbol of the magical circle she casts about herself and from which she draws power in order to enchant and transform men into pigs.

In this act the Goddess assumes human characteristics to entice men and then "unman" them. Perhaps Circe can be seen as the ancestral archetype of the *femme fatale* of the turn of the century. She is also human when she sings at the loom, a traditional feminine activity. But her domesticity hides perhaps another spell, for the weaving of the loom is in mythology a powerful metaphor for the creation of the world. The threads of destiny and time were spun and the world continuously woven. Her singing at the loom is therefore a symbol for her creative power. Her weaving does not affect the substance, but transforms the men with the freedom to transform them back into men at her will. They remain "untouched" at their core, their hearts at the periphery of the real and in this "mid-existence" she shows her sorceress nature, for she lives at the edge of the world – not completely evil nor completely good.

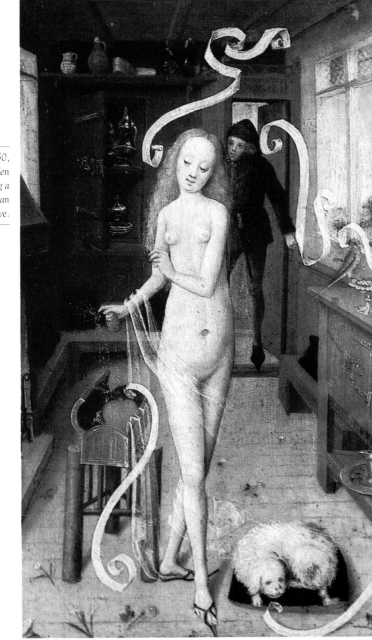

" Love Spell," c. 1450, Lipsia, Museum der Bildenden Kunst. A sorceress weaving a magic spell to bind her man with the threads of love.

The Archetype of Circe

HE WOMAN WITH Circe's qualities is a queen of magic. Standing alone within her own circle, she enchants existence into playing with her. The root of Circe's sorcery is the knowledge of the effect that a feminine charm has upon men. The ambivalent and potent character of the creator and destroyer archetype in the feminine psyche is an ever-present trait in every woman and it represents a great threat to a man. Circe lives therefore in every woman at the moment of seduction. The image of the woman as a demonic figure does not stem, as a rule, from the actual experience that a man has had in the relationship with a woman. It is derived from the man's fear that she will enchant him with her magic and transform him into "the pig he really is"! This point perhaps needs some explanation: there is an innate abhorrence in all of us toward our most primary instincts. The sexual drive a man feels when he sees an attractive woman is most often disguised in a more elegant approach. A man may not want to appear in the eyes of a woman as an "animal driven by his most basic instinct." The fear is that the Circe woman will magically see through the man's sophistications, guess his true feelings and use them in a manipulative way to transform him into a solely instinctive creature.

The Circe quality in a woman is the reflection of the feminine nature-spirit which inhabits the soul of every man. She represents, so to speak, his feminine instinct. Circe is the symbol of the demonic, non-human Goddess and she gives a man a taste of non-human Eros in all its power, of all irrational passion, both deeply satisfying and terrible at once. In ordinary life, a man does not meet his feminine instinct, for it is repressed by disciplined thinking and socially trained will. The feminine instinct as represented by Circe acts upon him directly from the unconscious, approaching him in his most intimate moments, like a traitor assaulting him in the night. The man distrusts this attack more than anything else in himself, and, when seized by this force, he unconsciously attempts to control the situation by depreciating the woman.

Ordinarily, a woman does not experience herself as demon and as a sorceress. The Circe woman, however, is fully aware of a deeper, perhaps darker, instinct which lives in recesses of her feminine psyche. The Circe woman has had the courage to look within and to bring to light an untamed force which is in reality shared by all women. She is aware of her ambivalent nature, living a polar existence between the conscious character she presents to others and the more erotic impulses and thoughts inherited from the non-human Goddess. Her magic is the ability to stand as master between the movements within her and in the world without.

In today's civilized world, women may find that they have separated themselves from their instincts by domesticating them to such an extent that the erotic attitude toward the social and domestic relationships has become organized and conventional. The woman's relationships may, as a result of this trend, feel stale and infertile, which causes suffering to be "cut off" from the inner source of life. The Circe woman has not made the clear cut between instinct and convention. She, therefore, lives an enriching and deeply satisfying life. Her relationships are led by instinct and she never hesitates in opening her heart to the deep feelings produced by contact with others. She seeks intimacy and never flees from the effects the other sex has upon her.

The Circe woman lives in a magical world in which she invites others to partake of her sorcery. She may be the kind of woman who makes others welcome in her own house, inspiring in them a feeling of warmth which causes them to open their hearts and reveal their secrets to her attentive ear. Her presence and modes may cause an alchemical transformation in other people. She may, for instance, make others feel at ease and in touch with their instincts. The Circe woman is often an expert of the energies which govern the body and she may be perhaps a doctor, an acupuncturist or a physiotherapist. Her touch and instinctive knowledge of the body in these cases help the patient to overcome the pain or illness easily and effortlessly.

"Isabella" by Sir John Everett Millais, 1849, Walker Art Gallery, Liverpool. The cooking of food can be seen as a metaphor for an alchemical transformation of raw material into an ecstatic substance which brings those who partake of it into a dimension which trascends ordinary reality.

The archetype of the creator and destroyer works in the Circe woman as a tool for physical transformation, in which the focus of the mind is brought from the rational to the instinctual plane.

The Circe woman is deeply feminine and has great care of her home and surroundings. As in the myth, she loves to prepare and offer food which is so good it almost resembles an ecstatic substance, a drug of the palate. In this aspect, we are reminded of the character of Babette, the French cook in Isak Dinesen's short story *"Babette's Feast"*.[32] In the story, a small Danish community of elderly people, who live in a far away village, are invited to supper by two sisters, daughters of the late deacon. Their father had held the community together by his religious fervor and enthusiasm for the word of God, always inspiring everyone to mutual respect and neighborly love. The night of the supper is the anniversary of the deacon's death and the two sisters are hoping to be able to bring back during the feast the lost feelings which held the community in harmony when the father was alive. Babette offers to buy the food herself, using the money won in a lottery, on the condition that the two sisters will not inquire of the strange activities which go on in the kitchen. On the night of the feast, the guests sit around the laden table and as soon as they taste the first spoonfuls of Babette's soup they start bickering bitterly about each other's offensive modes of behavior over the years.

As they indulge in the following courses of Babette's food, the guests become more and more at ease with themselves and with each other. Old grudges give way to genuine feelings of love and care. By the end of the evening everyone feels as if she or he had just entered paradise: free from emotional burdens, able to fly with the expression of their true emotions. Babette is the perfect example of the Circe woman: through the magic of her food she has destroyed the upper crust of the guest's behavior, bringing to light in its stead a truer, more genuine relationship, as if she had performed a sorcery.

A woman may activate Circe's archetype within her by learning to apply the "Goddess-given" magical touch to feminine activities in which she can exercise her transformative power. These might include spinning, weaving, cooking, massaging, curing. The archetype of Circe may be invoked by performing one of these activities as though it were a ritual in honor of the Goddess, placing special attention on the movements of the hands as if weaving magic rather than performing a mechanical act, and in exchange the Goddess will grant an assurance of success. There are moments in every woman's life when the archetype is invoked naturally. It may be in preparing a romantic candle-lit dinner for a lover, or the stroking of her child to comfort him in sickness. By using the instinct and by focusing on a magical result, magic is achieved. But any activity which involves using the hands as though they were a magic wand can induce the call for the power of the Goddess, even lighting the fire in the hearth. Once a woman can feel her own instinct as a guide to an activity, she can then expand, drawing a magical circle around all her activities, thus caring for her home or environment in the same magical way as she massages a body or prepares food.

Medea – the Murderess

THE myth of Medea becomes complete when the texts of two classical Greek authors, Homer and Apollonius, are considered. Homer recounts the myth, whereas in Apollonius's play dedicated to her, we hear the plea of a woman who could be our own contemporary. Medea was a Goddess and a Queen of Colchis, who spoke sagely through a "deathless mouth." She was also an expert in sorcery.

"Now, Medea, was the only surviving child of Aeetes, the rightful king of Corinth, who when he emigrated to Colchis had left behind as his regent a certain Bunus. The throne having fallen vacant, by the death without issue of the usurper Corinthus, son of Marathon, Medea claimed it, and the Corinthians accepted Jason (the husband of Medea) as their king. But, after reigning for ten prosperous and happy years, he came to suspect that Medea had secured his succession by poisoning Corinthus, and proposed to divorce her in favor of Glauce, the Theban, daughter of King Creon.

Medea, while not denying her crime, held Jason to the oath he had sworn at Aea in the name of all the gods,[*] *and when he protested that a forced oath was invalid, pointed out that he also owed the throne of Corinth to her. He answered, 'True, but the Corinthians have learned to have more respect for me than for you.' Since he continued obdurate, Medea, feigning submission, sent Glauce a wedding gift by the hands of the royal princes – for she had borne Jason seven sons and seven daughters – namely, a golden crown and a long white robe. No* sooner *had Glauce put them on, than unquenchable flames shot up, and consumed not only her – although she plunged headlong in the palace fountain – but King Creon, a crowd of other distinguished Theban guests, and everyone else assembled in the palace, except Jason, who escaped by leaping from an upper window.*

At this point Zeus, greatly admiring Medea's spirit, fell in love with her, but she repulsed all his advances. Hera (Zeus's wife) was grateful: 'I will make your children immortal,' said she 'if you lay them on the sacrificial altar in my temple.' Medea did so, and then fled in a chariot drawn by winged serpents, a loan from her grandfather Helius, after bequeathing the kingdom to Sisyphus." [33]

* Jason had sworn by all the gods of Olympus to keep faith with Medea for ever.

Above: "The End of a Kingdom" by Paul Delville.

The myth of Medea presents a riddle of Greek mythology in that the Goddess is a *divine Murderess*. The main difference between Circe and Medea is the difference between the net inside which Circe draws her victims, and the knife with which Medea slays, even if the murder of her children is intended to renew and rejuvenate their lives.

The tragic expression of the feminine nature represented in this myth is perhaps condensed in the words of Medea found in the play by Apollonius :

"It was everything to me to think well of one man,
And he, my own husband, has turned wholly vile.
Of all things which are living and form a judgment
We women are the most unfortunate creatures.
Firstly, with an excess of wealth it is required
For us to buy a husband and take for our bodies
A master. For not to take one is even worse.
And now the question is serious whether we take
A good or a bad one. For there is no easy escape
For a woman, nor can she say no to her marriage.
She arrives among new modes of behavior and manners,
And needs prophetic power, unless she has learned
at home,
How best to manage him who shares the bed with her.
And if we work out this all well and carefully,
And the husband lives with us and lightly bears his yoke,
then life is enviable. If not, I'd rather die.
A man when he is tired of the company in his home,
goes out of the house and puts an end to his boredom,
And turns to a friend or companion of his age.
But we are forced to keep our eyes on one alone."

(Medea, 228-247) [34]

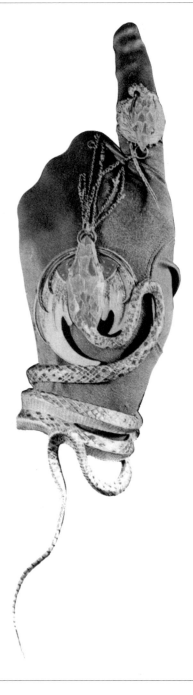

Medea gives in the above passage the reasons for her inflexible decision to murder her children, who had represented the continuance of married life, but who, after the treason of Jason, have become the medium through which she can regain her power by sacrificing them on the altar of immortality. Her desperate plea echoes the relationship of any modern woman who has chosen a man in love, with whom she envisages a prosperous future in which they commonly share their social power, but who is sadly let down when he grows tired of love with her and walks out in search of another.

Medea's myth centers around love and the deep wounds provoked by its excesses and desires to combine power with love.

> *"When love is in excess*
> *It brings a man no honor*
> *Nor any worthiness.*
> *But if in moderation Cypris comes,*
> *There is no other power at all so gracious.*
> *O Goddess, never on me let loose the unerring*
> *Shaft of your bow in the poison of desire.*
> *Let my heart be wise,*
> *It is the god's best gift.*
> *On me let mighty Cypris*
> *Inflict no wordy wars or restless anger*
> *To urge my passion to a different love.*
> *But with discernment may she guide women's*
> *weddings,*
> *Honoring most what is peaceful in the bed."*
> (Medea, 627-641) [35]

104

"Judith" by Gustav Klimt. Rejection of love is the most devastating of all deeds.

This piece in Apollonius's play is so modern in its content it might have been uttered by a contemporary woman, wounded in her misunderstanding of the wisdom of love.

"No, it was not to be that you should scorn my love,
And pleasantly live your life through laughing at me..."
(Medea, 1354-1355) [36]

It is the dominant woman's passionate grip on marriage speaking through Medea's mouth that seeks revenge from her husband who has discarded not only her, but blocked her ambitions to reign as queen in Colchis.

The Archetype of Medea

It is a popular belief that in the natural world of animals, the female of the species is more deadly than the male, for her passion is inflamed by the power of love.

T IS A POPULAR BELIEF that in the natural world of animals, the female of the species is more deadly than the male, for she is fiercer in love as well as in hate. The female is fecund and cruel, creating, cherishing and destroying. The Chinese call the full feminine force "yin." The yin principle, as seen by the Chinese, is everything shadowy, cool, dark, feminine and it is believed that this power commences in the autumn, overcoming the sun and giving way to the coldness and darkness of winter.

The Medea woman represents the yin primary principle of creation and destruction in the relationship with others. Unlike Kali who is an overall, powerful creator and destroyer of existence, and Circe, the expression of the innermost female instinct, Medea finds her fulfillment through a role. The Chinese identified the yin principle with the image of the female tiger. This animal is a fierce mother and she will glide

stealthily through the grass, waiting to leap upon the prey to bring back to her kittens with claws and fangs, yet looking all the while sleek, gentle and cat-like. If the kittens were to be killed by a hunter, the female tiger could easily murder this man with all her ferocity and her pain and her loss would be great and profound.

Medea is, like the tiger, a woman of roles; she is the queen of Colchis, which gives her social power. She is also, and foremost, the wife of Jason and the mother of their children. The identification with these roles is so strong that when her husband Jason falls in love with Glauce, Medea feels as if she no longer existed, for being a wife was very much part of her integrity. The only thing she can now do is to use her children as the tool of revenge. By sacrificing them on the altar of immortality, she grants herself the power

she had lost in the eyes of Jason. But by committing this murder she also, paradoxically, ends by her own hand the role of mother.

The woman who finds strong affinities with the Medea archetype is *the family woman*. She lives her life through the satisfaction of her husband, through the happiness and success of her children. She has, so to speak, no inner life of her own. Her focus is always to bring integrity and eternal happiness to her family. She gives and gains energy in the participation of the emotions which animate her cherished ones. She would do anything for them in a genuine and heart-felt outward movement. Her self-love is loving others. Her ambition is for the family to be together forever. The Medea woman is wholly dedicated to her home, to her children and to her companion.

"The Three Brides" by Jan Toorop, 1893. There are three types of marriage; marriage to the divine, marriage to the physical forces and marriage to an ideal.

It would be wrong to judge the Medea woman as naive, for she possesses rich inner resources, always injecting fresh and new energy into what she loves. Few women could be said to be radiating almost a holy happiness as does the Medea woman when she is surrounded by her family. She could become a good gynecologist, for instance, helping and counseling other women in their task of giving birth or bringing up children. She may be an excellent school teacher, who loves to involve the sharp minds of youngsters in the subjects she teaches. She could be a writer specializing in the subject of running homes and dealing with family problems. The Medea woman has perhaps gone out of fashion today, but she was for a long time in history the prototype of the "perfect woman."

We must not forget, however, that Medea represents the archetype of the creator and destroyer and, like Kali and Circe, her figure encloses a mystery. In the myth, Jason grows tired of loving her, leaves his home and begins a new relationship with Glauce. His action is political in its intent, for he undermines her own social power (he states that the Corinthians have learnt more respect for him than for her) and plans to join his kingship with the daughter of the king of another land. By the acquisition of greater power, Jason destroys the need to maintain the relationship with Medea. This is the key that turns the creator into the destroyer. For if the Medea woman cannot maintain her role of family woman, then she

must – her own instinct dictates it – kill, destroy and murder that which represented the family. She sets out in the myth to kill her own husband, whom she still loves, the new love Glauce, who represents a new beginning, a new family without Medea as the center of it, and she murders her own children who are her sole *raison d'etre*.

In the modern woman in whom the Medea archetype is working, this divine murder can be interpreted as her reaction at the end of a relationship. In today's world, the bondage of marriage is often no longer conceived as the *only* relationship one might have. Both men and women come together for a number of years and then depart when the relationship is no longer satisfactory, perhaps starting with another partner. Many women might therefore find themselves in the role of Medea at some point in their lives. When the husband finds a new love and walks away from the old one, every woman has a choice in how to come to terms with this painful event. The Medea woman attempts psychologically to *kill* her husband, in other words she chooses to end her role of wife by killing him as husband, lover and supporter of her family in her mind. Another kind of woman might have chosen to prolong her role of wife by asking to be maintained as such with alimony, paid to her by the lost husband. The Medea woman is singularly courageous, for in her destroyer mood she cuts with the sharp knife of her pain the link between her old role and the new reality.

When time comes for the children to leave home, the Medea woman *murders* them psychologically in order to set them free. In the myth the children are granted eternal life. Here again, every woman has the choice of either continuing the role of mother, entrapping thus the children who have left to find something new, or to cut the relationship and to start a new life by herself.

The Medea woman is remarkable in her features for she recognizes the patterns of past and future, and even though she deeply identifies with the loved ones, her wisdom is such that she sets them free at all costs. She creates a family and is capable of destroying it for the sake of freedom, never clinging to what was and is no more. Her pain is great, but the effect that such a woman has on the psychology of the loved ones is a demonstration of true love.

Medea's myth is probably Celtic in origin and tradition and it is believed that the Greeks borrowed it and incorporated it within their own mythology. However, the rituals in honor of Medea were considered too bloody for Hellenic taste and they were not adopted, remaining a tradition of the British Isles and Ireland, their original home. The main ritual of the Goddess occurred at mid-summer, when the sacred king, wearing a ram's mask, was slaughtered on a mountain top and his pieces stewed in a soup for the priestesses to eat. His spirit would then pass into one of them, to be born again in the next lambing season. In both Celtic and Greek mythology, Medea (or Medana as she was known to the Celts) was believed to preside over the cauldron of regeneration (where the body of the priest was "cooked" every year). In later times, the ancient Goddess was artificially canonized as a saint for her myth lived on in Christian times and she was associated with a regenerative well, whose waters were reputed to cure sore eyes. [37]

The woman who wishes to invoke Medea's archetype within her in order to aid the termination of a relationship, so that she may be free of it and able to start afresh, must focus on her own "regenerative" powers, as if she herself presided over a magic cauldron. By letting the instincts "boil," allowing their full expression in the form of rage or hurt, a woman may cure herself of painful attachments to the past. In this act, she is able to regenerate herself as if she died with the event that is so painful to her, with the consciousness that she must do this in order to be then able to start again.

Right: "The baleful Head" by Sir Edward Burne-Jones. The waters of a well, or cauldron, can be read in trance to seek the answers to the riddles of existence.

The Children of the Sea

HERE ARE MANY mythological figures which used to haunt popular imagination that are said to be the children of the sea. In mythology the sea represents the unconscious, a dark and fluid expanse that records ancestral memories which cannot be identified physically, as is the case with the children of the earth (mountains, trees, animals). The constant flow of the unconscious reveals the deepest fears of death by the irrational feminine power. As mentioned in the chapter on the psychology of myth, these female monsters often represent a man's *anima* shaped on the relationship with his mother which strongly affects his view of the world. The dread of the irrational and the fear of annihilation by unconscious forces are the root of the myths of female devouring monsters.

The Gorgons

The Gorgons were named Stheino, Euryale and Medusa, all once very beautiful. But one night Medusa lay with Poseidon, and Athene, enraged that they had bedded in one of her own temples, changed her into a winged monster with glaring eyes, huge teeth, protruding tongue, brazen claws and serpent locks, whose gaze turned men into stone.

Echidne

Half of Echidne was a lovely woman, half was a speckled serpent. She once lived in a deep cave among the Arimi, where she ate men raw, and raised a brood of frightful monsters by her husband Typhon: namely, Cerberus, the three-headed Hound of Hell; the Hydra, a many-headed water serpent living at Lerna; the Chimaera, a fire-breathing goat with lion's head and serpent body; and Orthrus, the two-headed hound of Geryon, who lay with his own mother and begot with her the Sphinx and the Nemean Lion.

CHAPTER FOUR

Lover and Seductress

Aphrodite, the Lover – The Archetype of Aphrodite – Hera, the Goddess of
Marriage – The Archetype of Hera – Salome, the Seductress – The Archetype
of Salome – Eve's Song of Temptation – The Archetype of Eve

Aphrodite

THE GODDESS OF LOVE is the first woman born out of the Sea of Creation. She brings the song of love to men and women.

"Uranus fathered the Titans upon Mother Earth, after he had thrown his rebellious sons, the Cyclopes, into Tartarus, a gloomy place in the Underworld, which lies as far distant from the Earth as the Earth does from the sky; it would take a falling anvil nine days to reach its bottom. In revenge, Mother Earth persuaded the Titans to attack their father; and they did so, led by Cronus, the youngest of the seven, whom she armed with a flint sickle. They surprised Uranus as he slept, and it was with the flint sickle that the merciless Cronus castrated him, grasping his genitals with the left hand (which has ever since been the hand of ill-omen) and afterwards throwing them, and the sickle too, into the sea by Cape Drepanum." [38]

Angelo Poliziano, a Florentine poet under the protection of Lorenzo de' Medici, took inspiration from Homer's *Hymn to Aphrodite* and wrote the most beautiful octaves ever to be dedicated to the Goddess of Love, which some years later were of inspiration to Sandro Botticelli for his famous painting *The Birth of Venus*.

In the mythical poem, the semen of Uranus fell into the sea and a gentle wind arose which transformed into a serpent and uniting with the fertile waves gave

The Lover

birth to Aphrodite (Venus in Roman mythology). The winds and waves carried her to Cyprus, the island which became her home, and, as she set her foot on the ground, flowers of all kinds sprang up.

She met the assembly of the gods and was received as one of them. Aphrodite was then free to choose a husband, unlike the other Goddesses who had married the men who had either raped (Demeter), abducted (Persephone) or seduced (Hera) them. She chose Hephaestus, whom she cuckolded many times.

Aphrodite wore a magic girdle which caused those who saw her to fall immediately in love with her. Her possessiveness of this gift made her most unpopular with the other Goddesses of Olympus, for she was jealous of her position – a metaphor perhaps for woman's desire for sexual attractiveness. She tempted men and gods alike into her bed of roses, whenever her husband was out of sight. A fleet of cupids obeyed her orders and traveled to the world of humans and, by shooting arrows into their hearts, made men and women fall in love with one another. This facility for providing the desire for sexual union finds much space in today's popular fiction and the many forms of "aphrodisiacs."

Aphrodite, the Goddess of Love and Divine Beauty, brings the song of love to all men and women. Page 116: Capitoline Aphrodite. This page: Medici Venus. The Romans imported the myth of Aphrodite to Italy and re-named the Goddess Venus.

Aphrodite's magic surrounds all those touched by it, man or god, in a golden cloud. The Goddess represents the transcendence of love from the temporal to the eternal plane. Here the Venus of Pompeii is portrayed.

Aphrodite did not bear any children to Hephaestus, but became the mother of numerous off-spring conceived out of wedlock. She had three children with Ares, the God of War: Harmonia, a daughter, and two sons, Deimos (Terror) and Phobos (Fear).

The relationship between Ares and Aphrodite is a symbol for the union of the two most uncontrollable passions – love and war – of mankind, which can either result in harmony or in terror and phobias. From her affair with Hermes was born the bisexual God Hermaphroditus, who inherited both their names, the beauty of both parents and had the sexual characteristics of them both.

The Goddess of Love also had relationships with mortal men. In some myths men who had asked for her help received her full graces, or, in other tales, she might develop a sudden passion and take the form of a human maiden for a time to seduce whomever she might fancy.

The profundity of Greek mythology lies in the images and symbols presenting something purely human – love – under the form of a divine Goddess. Let us imagine for a moment that love has two dimensions: the horizontal, enclosed between time and space, and the vertical, which represents the eternal. Human love, in this context, is on the horizontal plane, i.e. bound by time. We tend to seek permanency within a "relationship" – we bind it on a temporal level and thus often negate the presence of love in preference for such human needs as security or convenience. This "permanency" does not therefore fulfill the heart, which is seeking after the eternal, wishing always to be in love.

Aphrodite appears on the vertical plane, her love, unbounded by time, is eternal and deeply fulfilling. Aphrodite's magic surrounds all those touched by it, man or god, in a golden cloud. We speak of "falling in love," we do not say, as did the ancients, that we are under the spell of Aphrodite. What we mean is that we leave behind the rational plane, which is metaphorically placed higher – in the head – and "fall" into the instinctual domain.

Aphrodite is not a goddess of fertility, but of love lived out of freedom. It is said that in Lesbos, the poetess Sappho, a dedicated devotee of the cult of Aphrodite, named the river Aphrodisios in the Goddess's honor because women bathing there would reputedly become infertile. Aphrodite heals, through her magic, the hearts of men, and restores their unity with existence. Following her mythological birth, the primal unity which was broken by the bloody deed perpetuated by Cronus, is restored when the genitals of Uranus fall into the fertile sea and, there, the Goddess of Love is conceived, with healing and restoration as one of her inherited graces. Aphrodite appears when two halves are united and is thus the Goddess of wholeness, bringing the two polar opposites of male and female together within her golden light.

The magic of Aphrodite represents the mystery of transformation. Through her worship, man is elevated from human love to love eternal. The Goddess is the alchemical essence which unites the two most powerful forces of the universe, male and female, into completion. Through her, the eternal longing for unity and eternity is quenched.

The myth of Aphrodite is also a powerful symbol for the wisdom of love which rests within a woman's heart. A woman is always open to love, regardless of rejections or the behavior of men. A woman's "no," in matters of love is never a total rejection, whereas a man is generally less courageous, and more willing to run in the face of the "threat" of love.

Aphrodite is mistress of her own love life, something which many would love to emulate, and her freedom to be one in herself is derived from the wise knowledge that love is an essence which lies within one's heart and has nothing to do with permanency, nor stability of relationship. She is no reckless Goddess, as one would expect from the qualities she incarnates, but, on the contrary, is wise in all matters of love and relationships. Protective of her children, lovers and husband (whom she never divorced), she gives help to gods, Goddesses and humans alike. She incarnates, and we may believe this as an idealism, the divine touch of love, that which all humans desire, to let their hearts speak freely and simply, moment by moment, without serious sentimental bondages being created to hold and cling the beloved to our bosom forever.

Above: According to Greek mythology, Aphrodite was conceived in the fertile Aegean Sea from the union of a serpent with the waters. In this Greek terra-cotta from South Italy, the Goddess is flanked by cockle-shells to represent her marine origin. Page 121, top: "Waterbaby" by Herbert Draper Bottom: Microscopic photograph of a female hormone depicting, appropriately, its yonic shape. The female essence thus reverberates to the very core of female sexuality.

The Archetype of Aphrodite

HE ARCHETYPE OF APHRODITE becomes active in every woman at the moment in which she falls in love. It may be caused simply by a look, a fatal look that is, on the part of a handsome man and she will fall head over heels, recreating in her imagination the moment again and again thereafter. The touch of Aphrodite is irrational and is perceived as a magnetic attraction between a man and a woman, who would at that very moment run into each other's arms were they not held back by moral convention.

When a woman is touched by Aphrodite it may feel as if suddenly she was no longer herself. In the presence of the man in question, her cheeks may burn, the sentences of her speech become disjointed and meaningless, her eyes may shine brightly, her hands shake and she may wish that the earth would swallow her rather than let her continue playing the fool. But there is no escape from this gentle torture, for she will exude a magnetic energy which will envelop the man as well, catching him in the sticky web. One may be alarmed by such a strong reaction, for one may feel like a silly schoolgirl experiencing her first "crush."

The touch of Aphrodite is sometimes denied by women, for they are overcome by the sense of danger which making passionate love with a man they hardly know creates. Aphrodite then seeks revenge, by haunting the woman's mind with the sad thought that she

might have lost an important opportunity and that he might have really been the man of her life. Not to know is sometimes more blinding than to know.

It is very important for a woman to feel the touch of the Goddess of Love, for sensual enjoyment transforms her attitude towards herself, towards others and life in general. The joining of the male and female bodies can be seen as a mystical experience, for at the moment of orgasm the ego disappears and the self feels united, like a drop merging with the ocean. The calm and quiet after the tempest are the gifts that Aphrodite brings to the lover, for they are deeply soothing to the spirit. The body moves slower, the senses are more alert to sounds, shadows and light, the breathing is more regular and sleep is more profound. Most important of all is the sense of contentment that pervades the lover, within and without.

The archetype of Aphrodite works on the woman in love. It brings renewed beauty and freshness. Friends may remark on how good she is looking and may even dare ask the question – "Are you in love or something?" Aphrodite, as the Goddess of Love, is firstly in love with herself. The woman touched by her finds more time to dedicate to the care of her body, her hair, her way of dressing. Even her movements adopt a slower, flowing motion. She smiles so often, she is pleased to please.

The woman in whom the Aphrodite archetype is dominant is in love with being in love. She exudes a magnetic energy, attracting many men toward her who may believe she is in love with them. When they discover that this is only her natural way of being, they might be enraged with her for "leading them on," and blame her for being a tease!

The Aphrodite woman is very special in all respects. She is beautiful, her voice is soft and sensuous, her movements sleek and sinuous. She falls in love with a man and treats him like a god, dedicating her body, mind and soul to him. But it may be that when the man begins to show less attractive traits she leaves him and falls in love with another, repeating perhaps the pattern of easy and short relationships many times.

The Aphrodite woman lives moment by moment within a reality which is made exclusively of sensory perceptions. She does not share in conventional morality, for she believes everyone should be like her, and especially so other women. If she falls in love with a married man, for instance, she will seek to make him fall in love with her, oblivious of what the consequences might be of her sneaking into an established relationship. The Aphrodite woman often leaves behind her a track of hurt lovers and jealous wives. In this aspect, Aphrodite shows her terrible power. The pain of the heart is perhaps the most painful of all and many an abandoned lover contemplates psychological and sometimes even physical

The Renaissance image of the divine was found in the human expression of a body or a face. Here the divine essence of Venus is shown in the accompanying Cupids, who are winged, but nevertheless mischievously human.

suicide. When love goes, it is as if the sun itself had stopped shining. One is used to living, walking, talking, thinking, eating, sleeping, working, laughing and crying with the other. When the other is no longer there, a major psychological shift needs to occur in order to return to aloneness. If in her young age, the Aphrodite woman may mock these hurt people for not understanding the laws of love, time and experience teach her that love can be eternal and divine in a more stable, less unscrupulous relationship. The path along which the Aphrodite woman grows from her easy infatuations to a more mature self is by learning to look within, sorting the conflicting feelings which have lead her to fall in love compulsively. She will learn to gain emotional distance from her lovers, by finding other occupations in the world of work and friendships, both of which she may have set aside in her youth in order to pursue love affairs instead. And most important of all, the Aphrodite woman will learn the magic of the word "no," by learning to trust her feelings as well as her senses in the relationship with men, gaining thus wisdom which makes her able to enter a fulfilling and long-lasting rapport.

Cultivating Aphrodite is synonymous with cultivating beauty, physical ease and openness to love. The effect of the archetype may be felt as threatening to many for it opens the heart to change and new experiences. Moreover, falling in love creates chaos amongst the ordered things of life such as concentration on work and family.

In ancient Greece, women invoked the touch of the Goddess upon their hearts by performing the secret ritual of opening to her power. This entails the vision of oneself in the mirror of transformation offered by Aphrodite, which was believed to be adorned with fragrant red roses, the flowers of passion.

A woman may activate this archetype within herself by learning how to enjoy pleasure and opening her body to feeling with the alertness of her senses. Casting aside judgments about the frivolity and futility of such activities as flirting, dancing, having an affair, the woman may discover a vast, unexplored sea which lies within her waiting to be expressed. Taking time for herself or a holiday with her man away from it all are good ways to call on the power of Aphrodite, for love grows in a special climate. Caring for her body in a sensuous way, through massage or aromatherapy, also awakens the loving touch of Aphrodite. The Goddess demands personal attention in order to give to others.

Hera – the Goddess of Marriage

T HE myth of the Goddess:
"Hera, daughter of Cronus and Rhea, having been born on the island of Samos, was brought up in Arcadia by Temenus, son of Pelasgus. The Seasons were her nurses.

After banishing their father Cronus, Hera's twin-brother Zeus sought her out at Cnossus in Crete, where he courted her, at first unsuccessfully. She took pity on him only when he adopted the disguise of a bedraggled cuckoo, and tenderly warmed him in her bosom. There he at once resumed his true shape and ravished her, so that she was shamed into marrying him.

All the gods brought gifts to the wedding; notably Mother Earth gave Hera a tree with golden apples, which was later guarded by the Hesperides in Hera's orchard on Mount Atlas. She and Zeus spent their wedding night on Samos, and it lasted three hundred years. Hera bathes regularly in the spring of Canathus, near Argos, and thus renews her virginity.

To Hera and Zeus were born the deities Ares, Hephaestus, and Hebe." [39]

Hera's name is usually taken to have derived from the Greek word meaning "Lady" and having the Seasons as her nurses denotes her to be the inheritor of the ancient Mother Goddess, in her function of Lady of the Plants, protectress of the crops and giver of fertility. Hera was thus the Goddess of the Vegetative Year so that the three seasons, spring, summer and winter, her nurses in the myth, were sacred to her. She was worshipped under three different forms and sanctuaries throughout the year. In the spring, she was *Hera Parthenos*, the maiden. In the summer she became *Hera Teleia*, the fulfilled one, and in winter she was worshipped as *Hera Chera*, the widow. The moon – new, full, and old moon – was also a symbol for the three periods of agriculture under her protection. The three aspects of Hera represent the three phases in a woman's life, which were observed ritually by her priestesses and acolytes. The annual bath to restore her virginity seems to have been a purification ritual to restore her regenerative powers within the yearly cycle of plant reproduction, which the priestesses of her temple also emulated in a ritual.

The Archetype of Hera

Hera's marriage to Zeus:

"... and his (Zeus's) wife was equal to him in one thing alone: that she could still bestow the gift of prophecy on any man or beast she pleased.

Zeus and Hera bickered constantly. Vexed by his infidelities, she often humiliated him by her scheming ways. Though he would confide his secrets to her, and sometimes accept her advice, he never fully trusted Hera, and she knew that if offended beyond a certain point he would flog or even hurl a thunderbolt at her. She therefore resorted to ruthless intrigue...." [40]

There is a noticeable dichotomy between Hera the Protectress of the three phases of womanhood and the yearly cycle, and Hera the wife of Zeus. The marital relationship of the supreme God of Olympus and the Goddess of Marriage strongly reflects those barbarous customs of the Dorian Age, when women had been deprived of all their magical power, except that of prophecy, and came to be regarded as chattels, merely part of the husband's private property. The position of Hera as a mistreated wife creates the stage for both her positive and negative qualities.

ERA REPRESENTS A WOMAN'S yearning to be wed and to become a wife, to seek completion of herself with a faithful companion, whom she chooses for good. Her myth is also symbol of the endurance, loyalty and fidelity that a woman may feel for her husband.

When the Hera archetype is working in a woman's psyche, she will feel that the natural bond with one man is her only fulfillment. Therefore, even beginning as early as puberty, the Hera woman starts her search for a companion. The man she seeks needs to possess moral integrity, for she needs to be loved and respected in return for her feelings. He also needs to have a traditional view of marriage, to consider, in other words, his wife and the home as the center of his life. The Hera woman's ideal man is a man of power and social success, who excels at his career, for she is fulfilled through him, often not

"The Bride" by Marc Chagall. The archetype of Hera is activated when a woman is betrothed to a man with whom she will spend the rest of her life. The bride being led to the altar may feel like the wedding ceremony is an archetypal experience which deeply touches her heart.

"The Kiss" by August Rodin. The union of man and woman is sacred for it brings together all the opposing, but complementary, forces. The bodies of the lovers form a complete circle in which the two souls merge into one.

having any other ambition than being a good wife. When the Hera woman finds the man of her life she is bound to him for good. The day of the wedding is the most happy day and the marriage ceremony performed traditionally by a priest in a church is for her a mystical experience. The archetypal force that such a ceremony has upon her makes it into a divine marriage, in which the male and female are joined with the blessing of God.

From then on the Hera woman is the happy bride, waiting to hear her husband's steps to the door as he comes home from work, delighting in cooking delicious dishes for his enjoyment, and planning with him the furnishings of their cozy home. Her sexuality is deeply bound up with the feelings of love and respect she has for him. Love-making is often considered, with a truly positive attitude, as a duty to be performed with the partner, rather than the game of the senses that the Aphrodite woman plays.

Friendships and social life reflect the status of the Hera woman's married life. Other couples are visited, colleagues of the husband and their wives are invited to traditional parties and dinners. The Hera woman has no need of intimacy with other women or men friends, for she is wholly fulfilled in her role of wife. This setting can most often be found among the provincial bourgeoisie, which share the common belief that life is nothing more than marriage, work, children and eventually old age.

In the negative aspect, this archetype stems from a woman's deep-seated insecurity, a more or less unconscious fear that without a husband she may have no identity of her own in the eyes of society. Bound by tradition, such a woman sees her happiness fulfilled in traditional roles, namely that of wife and mother, and has perhaps no awareness of her own center which she tends to place in communion with a male partner. Thus her happiness or unhappiness, fulfillment or lack of it, freedom or imprisonment, depend totally and exclusively on the "other," on the husband.

Many women have a Hera trait in their character. The pleasures of married life, of making home and playing house, represent an unconditional attraction to woman, whatever the rules behind the game, even if she must remain inside the golden cage that results.

The Hera woman is so identified with her role of wife, that she may meet a few problems along the path of her life. She may consider her husband more highly than her own children. She will either side with him against the children, or ignore the child's true feelings, of which she is aware, and protect her husband's instead. This causes a deep hurt in the child, for he or she will feel the mother as a traitor and start competing with the father to gain her attention.

The Hera woman may find that love and the romance of married life no longer represent a central feature in her husband's concern. He may spend long hours at work and may never confide in her. She may therefore feel excluded and unable to fulfill her role completely. Even though she is aware that things are

> *The Hera woman takes pride in her family, to whose members she is emotionally attached to the extent that she lives in their function, her joy and satisfaction depending on theirs.*

not going well, she cannot find the strength in herself to face reality, but goes on, as if oblivious, with an apparently happy family life. This erodes her happiness slowly but surely, making her feel alienated from her own life, for she has never cultivated relationships nor activities that fulfilled her own self. Or, more sadly, the husband may have an affair and want to end the relationship with her. In this case, the Hera woman is totally unable to accept the rejection. Even after divorce, she may still feel and act as the rightful wife, interfering constantly with the husband and his new companion, as if nothing had changed. When this situation arises it is very difficult for everyone, for the Hera woman puts herself in a degrading situation by maintaining a dead role and by resorting to the psychological manipulation of her ex-husband, producing guilty feelings in him, thus compensating herself for the hurt done.

Unlike murderous Medea, who kills the new love of her husband, murders her children and forgets about her husband, cutting psychologically all bondages with them in order to start anew, the Hera woman cannot find the strength to conclude a chapter in her life. This inability causes a great deal of pain, not only to her, but to others as well. And this is where Hera's positive wisdom comes to her aid. In popular mythology, she was said to clad herself in darkness and undertake lonely journeys to the edge of the world, far and away from all the other Olympians, to recover from her husband's hurtful deeds. The mythological distance she

placed between herself, that is her unbounded need to "be" only with her husband, and reality (Zeus having numerous affairs) is the seat of her divine power. Hera is a figure of extreme compassion and in these long journeys she turned her compassion, understanding of herself and creative power, to heal her own heart. The swings of her amorous life, at times one with Zeus and at other times far and lonely, are a clear demonstration of the unresolved dichotomy within her character. The pull toward union and the distance of separation seem to echo the movements of the universe, as with the in and out of a human breath, they contain an element of the divine.

The longing for unity and the restoration of separation are the movements of a woman's heart and it may be that each cycle entails a different partner and that each time the movement is deeper, but the wisdom lies in the knowledge that there is no end to the ebb and flow of the current of life.

Pausanias, a Greek traveler and geographer who recorded ancient sacred rites for posterity, said that Hera was worshipped by her devotees as Child, Bride and Widow and that in her temple she passed endlessly through these three cycles, renewing her eternity at the end of each one. Hera's priestesses bathed yearly in a holy spring in order to maintain their purity intact.

The modern Hera woman is, as the Goddess in ancient Greece, easily identifiable, for hers is a vocation for the sacred union of marriage. She may therefore have been physically pure before the wedding, happy as a wife for a long time and living in memory of her dead husband as a widow. Many women may feel that the archetype is working within them when they start to long for settled, uncomplicated family life. Perhaps they may have fled from sentimental commit-

ment until then, and might have chosen unmarriable men as companions. Such unions may have proven in the long-run to be unfulfilling. When a woman realizes that committing herself to a man does not mean the death of her own freedom, but rather placing her center in communion with someone out of love, then the Hera archetype has been activated within her. The celebration of marriage and the commemoration of the happy day in the years to follow strengthens the bondage between the man and the woman, renewing their common desire.

If a woman has entered a fulfilling relationship with a man, and is torn between getting married to him or not, she may call on the powers of the Goddess to help her with this important decision. She may, for instance, move into a new house with him and face life as if she was taking on the responsibility of two lives instead of just her own.

Playing the role of wife as a game with Hera's help may turn out to be more pleasant than she thought and she may thus be convinced to take the step toward the fulfillment of the archetype.

Salome – the Seductress

Herod loved his daughter Salome not with fatherly love, but in the way a man looks and loves the body of a woman. During a feast which he held in his house, he wished to show Salome's beauty to all the guests. He thus decreed that if she danced the Dance of the Seven Veils to please him, she could ask whatever she wished for. Salome danced to please her father in circles at the furious beat of drums, and at each circle she shed one veil until she remained totally undressed.

She then asked for the head of John the Baptist to be served to her on a silver plate. John the Baptist was being kept in Herod's prison and had not returned Salome's love, for his heart was with God. Herod, unable to consume his passion for his daughter, gave in to her murderous wish.

THE Bible presents the myth of Salome as an opportunity to expose Herod's incestuous desire and his daughter's sinful and blood-thirsty nature. But Salome's Dance of the Seven Veils is in fact an allegory for the sacred drama of the life, death and resurrection of the King of Fertility and the journey that the Goddess undertakes into the underworld in order to restore him to life. In the same countries which had venerated the Goddess Ishtar and ritually worshipped the death and resurrection of her lover Tammuz, the myth of the Eternal Return lived on in the tale of Jesus, and many myths with the same topic were recorded in Christian parables, even though the original meaning became totally lost with the centuries.

Salome means "peace" (Shalom) and was the name given to the priestess impersonating the Goddess in her descent to the underworld. Passing through the seven gates in the temple of Jerusalem, which meant House of Peace, she removed one of her seven garments at each stage. [41] The seven veils represented the seven layers of earthly appearances or illusions, falling away as one approached the Mystery of the deep. The death of John the Baptist was a ritual sacrifice. Some early Christian sects ignored Jesus and believed John the Baptist to be their true king. As a "chosen one" John the Baptist may have been the one to play the role of surrogate king in the ritual of the eternal return, and his blood may have been required to fertilize – baptize – the land. John was beheaded, a common practice in the sacrificial worship of the Goddess, which is still carried out today in some Eastern temples, although the heads are of animals, and not men.

The beheading of John the Baptist in the myth of Salome is a symbol for a ritual sacrifice carried out in Asia Minor in Biblical times. John the Baptist, believed to be by some the true Messiah, may have been the chosen one to play the role of surrogate king in the ritual of the eternal return. His blood fertilized – baptized – the land.

The Archetype of Salome

WHEN A WOMAN IS seducing a man within the intimacy of the bedchamber she may feel like Salome. This moment is felt by both partners as an archetypal experience and is recorded in memory as a powerful and fulfilling event. We always remember the "first time" with a lover. At that moment, the body and the psyche of the woman becomes a medium through which powerful forces are channeled. The union of male and female can be seen as a *unio mystica* for it is the joining of two polar opposites. The dance that leads to it is a gathering of opposite energies as powerful as the growing of a tidal wave in the sea. The two lovers are sharply in tune with one another: movements, smells, looks reflect the magnetism back and forth, from the woman to the man, from the man to the woman in a crescendo which cannot be reached in any other way.

The symbol of the shedding of the seven veils in the myth can be seen as a metaphor for the "nakedness" of the lovers. The moment of seduction is a moment of truth for one shows oneself as one is. Stripped of clothes and worldly roles, the lover gives him or herself in humility and purity. There is no hiding from the eyes of the other, and the acceptance of the partner towards who we really are is almost a divine gift, which is sought again and again.

The beheading of John the Baptist in the myth is a powerful symbol for leaving the plane of reason and entering the sensual plane. The lover is beheaded by Salome, for it is always the woman, and this is a mathematical formula, who is the one to bring the man away from reason into the heart. Seduction cannot take place if the mind is active as it is in other moments outside love. The head of John the Baptist was presented to her on a silver tray. Silver reflects images and this mythological symbol stands for the need of the mind to become a mirror of the emotions at the moment of seduction. All thoughts stop and there is only the witnessing of sensual perception. This state can be felt in meditation. But a woman can bring it about in a man whenever she wants. This is perhaps why Salome has been seen as a demoniacal figure by the morally oriented fathers of the church.

"The Apparition" by Gustave Moreau. The head of John the Baptist surrounded by a halo of light appears to Salome in a vision. Love and sexual desire rises within like a tidal wave, sweeping far and away the rational mind and centering the powers of the body and psyche on the sensory perceptions. The transformation that thus occurs has magical effects, for both the woman and the man become aware of the union of the ego with the self.

Eve's Song   of Temptation

"The Lord Yahweh said to the woman, 'What is this that you have done ?' The woman said, 'The serpent beguiled me and I ate.' Yahweh said to the serpent, 'Because you have done this, cursed are you above all cattle and all beasts of the field. Upon your belly you shall go, and you shall eat dust all the days of your life. I will put enmity between you and the woman, and between your seed and her seed; he shall bruise your head and you shall bruise his heel.'

Thus Yahweh cursed the woman to bring forth in pain and be subject to her spouse.
And he cursed, also, the man who had come to the tree and eaten of the fruit that she presented.
'In the sweat of your face, you shall eat bread,' he said, 'till you return to the ground. For out of it you were taken. You are dust, and to dust you shall return.'"
(Genesis 3:13 – 19)

The myth of Eve is perhaps the richest of all myths, for the curse of the Lord on her disobedience sets the seal of patriarchy and centuries of female repression in the new age that followed millennia of worship of the Great Mother Goddess.

The biblical title of Eve, Mother of All Living, is a title which had been widely used in the Mesopotamic regions as the name of the all-powerful Goddess. It is still believed nowadays in the Hebrew faith, that the name of God, YAHWEH, cannot be pronounced as it manifests the full creative powers of God the Creator. The secret of God's name of power, the Tetragrammaton, was that three-quarters of it invoked not god, but Eve. YHMH, came from the Hebrew root, HWH, meaning both "life" and "woman," in Latin letters E-V-E. With the addition of an I, it amounted to the Goddess's invocation of her own name as the Word of Creation, which had been a common idea in Egypt and other regions where the Mother Goddess reigned supreme. The ancients believed in fact that by pronouncing the name of the Goddess one could invoke her power and she would become manifest. The same belief is still held in Tibetan Buddhism in which mantras such as OM, the soundless sound, are chanted in meditation in order to unite the Self to the powers of the Universe.

According to Gnostic scriptures it was Eve, and not God, who created Adam. He is said to have been made out of blood and clay: it was a common practice in the worship of the Goddess and the God of Fertility, to shape a god-like man made out of clay to represent the power of creation of the Goddess. The legend of Adam's rib out of which Eve was created is now popularly known to be a patriarchal inversion of the myth of the hero-god born from the Goddess Earth, who returned to her to be reborn, which had pre-existed Christianity and from which the new faith had drawn. For Adam and Eve are the children of Mother Earth, out of her they had been taken and to her they would

Eve's song of temptation is a powerful symbol for the vessel of transformation represented by woman: by eating the apple offered to him by Eve, woman, Adam, man, may attain the divine.

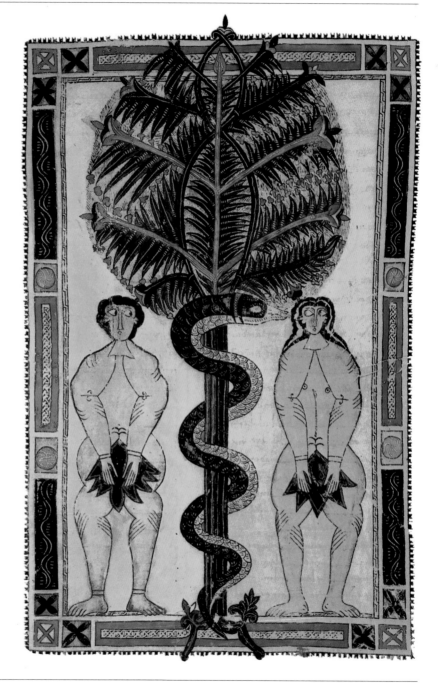

return (the dust mentioned in the quote from the Bible is a metaphor for the earth). There is clear and adequate evidence throughout the biblical text reporting the Fall from Paradise, that the Lord Yahweh was only a manifestation of the creative power of the serpent.

The symbol of the serpent was inherited from earlier mythologies in which the Mother Goddess took as spouse a serpent and, after uniting with him, gave birth to all living things.

Gnostic texts again report that Eve, meaning Life, was "the Good Spirit, the Thought of Light called by him 'Life' (Hawwa)." [42]

With the advent of Christianity, the ancient myth of the Goddess of All Things and of her lover, who dies periodically, to resurrect and create life anew, was split into two. On the

one hand, Eve, the inheritor, according to Gnostic and early Christian texts, of the full power of the Goddess, was stripped of her power of creation, and was transformed by patriarchy into a vessel for pregnancy and birth. The curse that the male God imposed on her, to bear children in pain, was to become the destiny of millions of women for centuries. She was the one who brought on death, as the ancient Goddess had done, except that the power to resurrect the beloved god-king was taken away from

her and became the attribute of a male god. The Church Fathers saw Eve as Death incarnate, and their manipulation of the original myth had disastrous consequences for the psychology of women and men. The splitting of the powers of the Goddess between Eve, as the sinful one, and God, the savior, is the root of the phobia of the Church Fathers against woman, for she was solely identified with the dark force of no return. The sin committed in paradise with its consequent fall, is that the two polar divinities who created life together have been split into two opposing halves, and bliss and eternal life can only be restored when the two primal forces of creation are united again.

The condemnation of Eve must have reflected some truth. Early Gnostic texts state that women of the ancient world were disposed to ignore the God who had cursed their sex and progeny forever. In fact, without the orthodox myth of Eve the sinner and the Fall, the basis of Christianity would suddenly become too fragile. "Take the snake, the fruit-tree, and the woman from the tableau, and we have no Fall, no frowning Judge, no Inferno, no everlasting punishment – hence no need of a Savior. Thus the bottom falls out of the whole Christian theology." [43]

The Archetype of Eve

I F WE SET ASIDE THE rhetorical meanings of this myth, told countless times by the fathers of the church, we may be able to extricate a deeper meaning which touches the heart of every woman. Adam and Eve had been created by God as reflections of his own self. However, they were human, not divine like God. While living in bliss in the garden of Eden, Eve was tempted by the serpent into eating the fruit of the tree of knowledge, an act God had forbidden the human couple from doing lest they should meet his full wrath. After Eve partook of the forbidden fruit she found it so delicious that she tempted Adam into eating the apple as well. This is the kernel of the sin. The knowledge that the tree represents is the knowledge of the divine, in other words, enlightenment. This knowledge was jealously guarded by God for it was only his own. By eating the fruit, Eve became aware that the knowledge was not informative, but transformative, bringing her from the human plane to the divine. When Eve offered the apple to Adam she offered him the possibility of becoming God himself, in other words, enlightened.

In many Eastern religious currents, man attains truth through the medium of a woman. In the Tantra vision, for instance, the teacher, the guru, is a woman. She leads the man away from reason and brings him through sexual ecstasy into true knowledge. This concept may seem alien to us, for Western women have been so conditioned into feeling guilty about the temptation which has been misunderstood and manipulated for centuries, that they cannot place the force of this archetype within them. Perhaps every woman is aware of her intuitive knowledge, of her attunement with natural law. She may not be aware, however, of the extent of her power and of the ways in which she can experiment with it. A woman who has entered disciplehood is initiated to the knowledge of her soul, and her search is to find the divine within herself. This concept is perhaps nowadays more popular than it was only two or three decades ago, when there was no understanding whatsoever of the inner search.

The archetype represented by Eve is within the chapter of love. The way of a woman is the way of love, it is her climate, her way of existence. If the modern woman lets love grow into her heart, if it becomes her meditation, then God will be growing of His own accord. If a woman misses the experience of love as divine, then she will miss God and all.

The message of love brought by woman in every task she performs, in every movement of her body, in every word she speaks, could become a living religion for humanity, for she is the medium through which such a message is given.

CHAPTER FIVE

The Mother

The Miracle of Motherhood – The Mother Archetype as Symbol of Eternal
Return – The Full Moon as Symbol of the Mother Goddess – Queen Isis –
The Archetype of Isis – The Mysteries of Eleusis: Demeter and Persephone –
The Mother Archetype of Demeter – The Daughter Archetype of Persephone –
From Mother to Saint: The Transition between Pagan Worship and Christian
Faith – The Virgin Mary, Mother of God – The Archetype of Mary

The Miracle of Motherhood

HE ARCHETYPE OF THE MOTHER is perhaps among the most complex of mythological and psychological concepts. It crystallizes such ideas as life within the womb, existence in darkness outside a time frame, the trauma of birth, the "oneness" of mother and child, the longing for a return to the womb's enclosing existence, the instinctual knowledge of the origin of mankind.

Conception, pregnancy and giving birth represent an important threshold in the archetypal history of a woman. The physical phenomenon of pregnancy is almost miraculous in its essence, for woman multiplies herself into another being and becomes the channel for bringing another soul to life. For nine months she creates matter, shapes a body, brings substance within herself like an alchemist transforming essence into living matter. During the pregnancy months a woman glows, her pupils may dilate and she may radiate beauty, happiness and blissfulness. Like a true master of magic, the more she gives the more she receives creating a spell-binding circle between her psyche and body which may transport her to an apex of fulfillment she may find difficult to equal under other circumstances.

One of the most fundamental understandings of psychology is that many of the difficulties we encounter in adult relationships with others find their root in our childhood. The first seven years of a child's development are fundamental for later growth: the relationship with the parents, especially that with the mother, the view of the world, fears, desires and understandings are all shaped in this early period. These childhood experiences mold our personality and our way of relating to the world. Psychological trends that we may carry for years and years which form a "knot" in our lives stem from this period. It may take years of unraveling with the help of a psychologist before the root cause of the problem is discovered, or, worse still, it is never related to a childhood event and keeps haunting us like a malignant shadow until death. The role of mother, of initiator of a child into the world, is therefore of fundamental importance for she represents the feminine essence which shapes the intimate feelings for life and relations with others in the child's psyche. Through her eyes and senses the child will learn how to behave and rely on its intuitions. Both adult men and women retain many habits which were taught to them by their mothers, especially in the intimate sphere of home and family.

The human experience of birth and motherhood is thus catapulted into the macrocosm of myth and made into the law of all things; the earth becomes Mother Earth, water becomes the womb whence the cosmos originated. Every particle of existence is subject to the myth of the eternal return represented by the archetype of the mother: conception, birth, life, death and re-birth.

The mother is the first teacher. She opens the doors of good and evil through which she lovingly guides the child into existence.

The Mother Archetype

An archetype affects the personal unconscious, shaping it according to the force with which it is perceived. The analysis of symbols that appear to us in dreams, trance-like states, moments of intuition, help us to unveil the meaning of the archetype.

WE CAN ANALYZE an archetype according to two keys of interpretation. On one level it represents a psychological trend of the *collective* unconscious, a mode of response and behavior whenever the archetype is met, which is shared by many individuals throughout history. On another level, it affects the *personal* unconscious, bringing to light singular and particular psychological trends in the individual.

The mother archetype has perhaps the greatest impact on the collective unconscious of all the archetypes pertaining to the mythology of the Goddess, for it affects both men and women alike and not only in the private sphere, but it touches and influences their

as Symbol of Eternal Return

Painting, only guided by the unconscious, reveals symbols pertaining to our personal experience of an archetype. The mother archetype is an all-encompassing psychic force which may well be drawn as a circle with motifs in its center.

social and religious expressions.

The mythological figure of an all-powerful Mother Goddess is believed to be the first divine being with human characteristics to have been created by mankind. The mythology of the Mother finds its origins in prehistoric times and archaeological evidence testifies that this figure was for many centuries at the center of the religious and social structure of tribes and early communities throughout ancient Mesopotamia and Europe, from Spain to the Russian Urals. A series of powerful symbols accompany her myth and these have been passed from generation to generation, from culture to culture, for millennia and have fundamentally shaped the Western religions of today. [44]

Among the symbols of the feminine deity of motherhood is the meeting of Heaven and Earth within the

body of the mother, for she incarnates human qualities and at the same time she is the vessel and instigator of the divine law by which all things are conceived, nurtured and brought to life. Women who became expectant mothers in ancient times were seen as incarnating and perpetuating the will of the celestial mother; their human destiny was a reflection of the law of the feminine principle.

The archetype of the mother is in our psyche a symbol for the archetypal place of origin. She represents the center which created us and to which we were once attached by the umbilical cord. After birth, when the umbilical cord is cut, the bondage persists in our psyche and emotions. Throughout mythology and the history of religions we find that men and women sought to express their link with the center of origin in terms of a link with the divine. Mountains, for instance, which may be seen to resemble the shape of the pregnant woman, were made sacred, for they were seen to join heaven to earth and be the manifestation for both divine and temporal principles.

Burial of the dead stems from the underlying belief that the body returns to the Mother (the earth is seen as the Great Mother) to await re-generation. The mythological and religious view of the destiny of mankind – birth, life, death and re-birth – closely followed the scheme of the vegetative year divided into seasons of seeding, growing of the crops, harvest and death during the winter-time. [45] In fact, Western religions are an inheritance of the belief systems of the agrarian communities of the past which saw life as cyclic and dependent upon the feminine principle of regeneration which united periodically with the male principle of creation and fertility. The ancients believed that every creation was a reflection of an act of cosmogony; it was a repetition of the divine creation of the world and of life itself. The new creation of plants and crops each spring is a symbol for the regeneration of time, for life can start anew. The birth of a child is, of course, another manifestation of the same idea.

The Mother Goddess presided over agricultural festivities in order to ensure with her own fertility the fertility of the land and the continuation of vegetation and human life.

The Full Moon as Symbol of the Mother Goddess

THE moon is depicted, almost without interruption from the Neolithic period to Medieval art, in conjunction with the figure of the Goddess, and it is still found in contemporary Christian art close to the image of the Virgin Mary. [46] More than a poetic and inspiring metaphor for the gentle and mysterious powers of the night and the waning and waxing phases, the moon represents the firm principle of femininity, as the customs of peasants all over today's rural Europe testify. The months of the year for the agricultural communities remain thirteen as in ancient times, because the moon waxes and wanes thirteen times. No seed is planted, no field is ploughed, no harvest is gathered without considering the movements of the moon. Weather reports are cast accurately just by glancing at the position, at the phase of the moon and by feeling the breezes of the evening sky. The farm animals are left outside or gathered inside the safety of the stables depending on what the moon "looks like." In many languages the word "lunatic" derives its meaning from the influence that the moon has upon the moods of men, women and animals.

The full moon stands at the center of the lunar cycle, between the waxing and waning phases.

Its rotundity and completion have come to represent through the ages the full expression of a woman's potential in pregnancy and motherhood. The body of a woman reaches its physical apex during pregnancy and childbirth, for this time requires the greatest physical strength and integrity.

Many women today are choosing to give birth in a more natural way, without the use of modern drugs designed to annihilate pain, because such methods also tend to numb the mother's natural connection with birth and there is also risk of psychological damage to the child.

Mary Magdalene was a sacred prostitute, she mediated between the world of the divine and the world of humans. There are myths that depict Mary Magdalene's ability to perform miracles. One tells of when she saw and spoke to the risen Christ, as it is believed she was the first to do. She hurried off to tell the other disciples. On her way, she met Pontius Pilate and told him of the wondrous news. "Prove it" Pilate said. At that moment a woman carrying a basket of eggs passed by and Mary Magdalene took one in her hand. As she held it before Pilate, the egg turned a brilliant red. To attest to the legendary event, in the cathedral which bears her name in Jerusalem stands a beautiful statue of Mary Magdalene holding a colored egg. The halo which surrounds her head is a symbol for the moon-given gift of sight into the mystical domain.

Mothers are learning to maintain their contact with the child during birth through the body's process of pain and contraction. Breath training during pregnancy serves as a natural aid for the body to cope with the pain. Woman has also, perhaps, become more aware of the moon as a symbol of the fullness of the experience of pregnancy, child-birth and motherhood.

Moon symbology lingers on nowadays in any case in Catholic countries such as Italy, France, Spain and Portugal, where the Virgin Mary, the mother of mothers, is sometimes called the Moon of the Church, Our Moon, the Spiritual Moon. A woman may count the length of the pregnancy term as the passing of nine moons, for it is believed that after the ninth lunar cycle the baby will for sure be born.

Left: The archetypal mother was often portrayed with many breasts to symbolize her cosmic nourishing power. Right: An Egyptian representation of Queen Isis wearing cow horns and the sun disc. In ancient Egypt, the cow was a sacred animal for its milk represented the nourishing power of the mother. Young princes were brought up exclusively on cow's milk in order to symbolically instill in them the stamp of the divine mother.

Queen  Isis

In Egyptian hieroglyphics Isis was called "the many-named," as the following passage from Lucius Apuleius describes. But Queen Isis of Egypt was foremost a divine mother and as such she was worshipped in many countries of Ancient Mesopotamia. Her powerful myth was inherited by the Greeks and also served as inspiration for the Christian image of the Holy Mother. *The Golden Ass* is perhaps the most comprehensive and inspired account of Queen Isis as representing the Great Mother Goddess of ancient times to be found in classical literature.

In the story, Lucius Apuleius wakes suddenly in the night and is seized by fear. The full moon, symbol of the mother and full expression of the feminine force, shines bright in the night sky. Lucius Apuleius thinks this is the most intimate and secret hour, when the Goddess is at her strongest and most puissant. He thus invokes her powers with a prayer and returns to sleep. Queen Isis appears to him in a dream and describes herself thus:

"Behold, Lucius, I am come; thy weeping and prayer hath moved me to succor thee. I am she that is the natural mother of all things, mistress and governess of all the elements, the initial progeny of all the worlds, chief of the powers divine, queen of all that are in Hell, the principal of them that dwell in Heaven, manifested alone and under one form of all the gods and Goddesses. At my will the planets of the sky, the wholesome winds of the sea, and the lamentable silences of Hell be disposed; my name, my divinity is adored throughout the world, in divers manners, in variable customs, and by many names. For the Phrygians that are the first of all men call me The Mother of Gods at Pessinus; the Athenians, which are sprung from their own soil, Cecropian Minerva; the Cyprians, which are girt about the sea, Paphian Venus; the Cretans which bear arrows Dyctinnian Diana; the Sicilians, which speak three tongues, Infernal Proserpine; the Eleusians, their ancient Goddess Ceres; some Juno, other Bellona, other Hecate, other Rhamnusia, and principally both sort of the Ethiopians which dwell in the Orient and are enlightened by the morning rays of the sun, and the Egyptians, which are excellent in all kind of ancient doctrine and by their proper ceremonies accustom to worship me, do call me by my true name, Queen Isis. Behold, I am come to take pity of thy fortune and turbulation; behold I am present to favor and aid thee; leave off thy weeping and lamentation, put away all thy sorrow, for behold the healthful day which is ordained by my providence." [(47)]

Queen Isis was born from the union of the Earth-god Seb and the Sky-goddess Nut and was thus venerated in ancient Egypt as the corn and fertility Goddess as well as being worshipped as the Mother of Mothers. She married her own brother Osiris and gave birth to their child Horus. According to Egyptian mythology, Isis finds wheat and barley growing wild and her husband Osiris introduces methods for their cultivation gaining wealth and gratefulness from his people. His brother plots the death of Osiris out of jealousy and succeeds in nailing him inside a coffer which he drowns in the waters of the Nile. Isis undertakes a long journey to the swamps of the river's delta (a metaphor for the underworld) in search of dead Osiris. In the meantime, the coffer containing the god's body floats ashore at Byblus where a fine erica-tree springs up suddenly enclosing the coffer in its trunk. When Isis arrives at Byblus, she pours scented ointment onto the tree-trunk and wraps it in linen. She leaves Byblus with the coffer containing her husband's body which she hides while she visits her son Horus. The jealous brother, however, finds the coffer while he is hunting wild boar and breaks it into fourteen pieces which he scatters all around. Queen Isis patiently finds each piece, molds it into the god's image with clay and entrusts it to the chief priest of the region where each piece is found. To each priest she says that what she is giving him is the whole of Osiris's body and as such it should be honored and worshipped for the ages to come. By her device Osiris is worshipped in all regions of Egypt.

The myth of Isis and Osiris is a powerful allegory for the eternal cycle of the alternation of the seasons. Osiris represents wheat, the main cereal in the Egyptian staple diet. His death was mourned in the winter, when the wheat stops growing. The springing up of the erica-tree is a metaphor for the sprouting of the grain in the fields in the spring-time. In the same fashion as Isis wrapped her beloved husband in linen, perfumed him with scented ointments and uttered powerful spells for eternal life, so the Egyptians copied the ceremonies and wrapped their dead into mummies, and placed them inside pyramids with food and worldly objects, believing that death was but a temporary rest in the cycle of eternity shaped by their gods.

The scattering of all the pieces of the coffer in which the god's body was contained is a symbol for the harvesting of the wheat.[48]

The Archetype of Isis

ISIS WAS VENERATED throughout ancient Mesopotamia as a queen who bestowed riches upon mankind and land alike. Her powers are both human and divine, for she conceived and brought up her child Horus to be a king of Egypt, and grieved her husband's death as a woman would. Her role of mother and companion to Osiris was sublimated to the mythical context of Egyptian religion, for her figure incarnates the seat of origin of all things and the center of female power.

The archetype of Isis represents the fully flowered power of a mother. There are different ways for a woman to experience this role, but when the Isis archetype is active she may feel that she is in touch with other-worldly powers. Pregnancy, childbirth and motherhood represent for the Isis woman a movement of her consciousness, a step toward the unveiling of her own personal feminine strength. The Isis mother stands at the center of existence, like an open passage for the flow of life and she is conscious that her act is the necessary repetition of the continuous regeneration of nature without which all living things would come to an end.

The Isis woman may therefore experience motherhood as the providing of a channel for a new life to be born, her more human feelings, such as pride for the baby and the desire for it to be uniquely hers and to be brought up according to the world-view she has set for herself, these things may be of secondary importance. The Isis mother will seek to maintain the child's individuality throughout its development, being careful not to stamp her own fears and desires upon the child's psyche.

Isis was venerated as a virgin-mother and she is often portrayed seated with Horus suckling at her breast, an image that was later to be borrowed by Christianity to represent the Virgin Mary. The Goddess's virginity is a symbol for her own individuality of character, being "one-in-herself".[49] The relationship of the Isis woman toward the father of the child is bound to be one of companionship, rather than of dependence. Like Queen Isis, she will always be a woman and a lover to him, keeping her roles of mother and companion to a man well defined and separate. When the Isis woman sets up a family it becomes her main concern and she will elevate its members to form part of the royal entourage, for she is a queen of female power and understanding. She intuitively knows her children and husband, perhaps more than they wish her to, for they may feel she sometimes breaks the laws of individual privacy in her eagerness for each of them to be "royal" and act according to her own view of life. She may overlook the fact that personal feelings and experiences are very much part of an individual's life and not separate from personal action.

On the other hand, if she decides not to form a

family, the Isis woman may be perfectly at ease as a single parent, caring for the child and providing all the comforts and sustenance herself. In this case, she will take on the role of father also, introducing the child into the unknown world of male mysteries in the same way as Isis in the myth when she undertakes the long journey in search of Osiris to the swamps of the Nile's delta.

The Mexican Moon Goddess Tlazolteoltl giving birth to herself, as "the old moon gives birth to the new." This is, strangely, a very powerful representation of the modern method of giving birth in a squatting position.

The kernel of the Isis archetype is the consciousness of being the seat of life, a woman's awareness of her own function of beginner, nurturer and medium for life to accomplish its means. This knowledge pervades through the character of the Isis woman, who owns the "Goddess-given" gift of mastery of her own destiny. The Isis woman knows, in other words, that her life and her role of mother are part of the great mesh which forms the pattern of existence. She is therefore reassured by this knowledge that her decisions are not a lonely cry, but are sustained by the very workings of nature. Her motherhood reminds her of the flowers opening their petals to receive the light of the sun, of the moon shining bright, of the stars and the whole cosmos echoing her life.

The ancient Egyptians held a ritualistic festival in honor of Isis at the time the Nile began to rise (the waters of the Nile were the only source of field irrigation, for the country is almost completely without rain). They believed that the Goddess was mourning the loss of her beloved and that her tears swelled the tide of the river. Sirius, the brightest of all the stars, appeared at dawn in the east, at about the time of the summer solstice. The Egyptians called it Sothis and regarded it as the star of Isis. It seemed that the great mother and Goddess of fertility had come to mourn her departed lover and wake him from the land of the dead. The rising of Sirius/Isis marked the beginning of the sacred Egyptian year. [50]

Cultivating the Isis archetype compels one to take an active interest in the observation of natural events as echoes of one's own state of being. The Isis mother may, for instance, develop an interest in astrology, reading in the positions of the stars at the birth of her baby important signs which will help the child's growth. Or she may wish to be close to the sea while pregnant, for its tides are reminiscent of the impending birth. When the Isis archetype is active, a woman feels naturally drawn toward the observation and recording of the phases of the moon, the movements of the stars. She may feel the effect of changes of weather, feeling like staying at home on a cloudy and rainy day, and like going out on a sunny day. The fluctuations in the atmosphere, the colors of the trees, the fragrance of flowers deeply influence the mood of the Isis woman, for she is deeply in touch with nature. Moving to a house in the countryside, where she can listen to the sounds of animals and to the wind rustling the leaves of trees at night, is a good way to open the psyche to the effect of this archetype.

The Mysteries of Eleusis – Demeter and Persephone

THE agrarian communities of the ancient world shared the wonder at the continuous regeneration of the plant life which formed their life's sustenance. The birth, life, death and re-birth of the cereals cultivated was celebrated by rituals and recorded in myths. The principle of renewal was personified by the Mother Goddess whose fertility granted the fertility of the land. The wheat was person-ified by a god who died each winter and came to life again each spring. The myths of the mother, therefore, resemble each other closely for they all center around the same principle of eternal rejuvenation. Whereas in Mesopotamia the mythical union of female and male, of the Goddess and her lover, was believed to propiti-ate the growth of the crops, Greek fancy embodied the same idea in the tenderer and purer form of the love of the mother Goddess Demeter for her daughter Persephone. The rites of Demeter were celebrated in September at Eleusis, a city-state in a flat expanse where wheat was cultivated, not far from Athens.

The oldest literary account of this myth is the Homeric *Hymn to Demeter* which is now believed to have been written in the seventh millennium before our era. It is easy to gather the personality of the two Goddesses behind the veil of the poetic context, trans-porting thus the impact of the myth onto a more per-sonal level.

The young Persephone was gathering roses and lilies, crocuses and violets, hyacinths and narcissuses, when the earth gaped and Pluto, Lord of the Dead, issuing from the abyss, carried her off on his golden car to be his bride and queen in the gloomy subterranean world. Her sorrowing mother Demeter, with her yellow tresses veiled in a dark mourning mantle, sought her over land and sea, and learning from the sun her daughter's fate, she withdrew in high dudgeon from the Gods and took her abode at Eleusis, where she presented herself to the king's daughters in the guise of an old woman, sitting sadly under the shadow of an olive tree beside the Maiden's Well, to which the damsels had come to draw water. In her wrath at her bereavement the Goddess suffered the seed not to grow in the earth, but kept it hidden under ground, and she vowed that never would she set foot on Olympus and never would she let the corn sprout until her lost daughter should be restored to her. Vainly the oxen dragged the plough to and fro in the fields. Vainly the sewer dropped the barley seed in the furrows of the earth. Nothing came up in the parched and barren soil. Mankind would have perished of hunger had not the God Zeus commanded Pluto to restore his bride Persephone to her grieving mother Demeter. The Lord of the Dead obeyed, but before he sent back Persephone he gave her to eat the seed of a pomegranate which ensured that she would return to him. Thus Zeus commanded that Persephone should spend two thirds of every year with her mother and the gods

of the upper world and one third of every year with her husband in the nether world, from which she was to return year after year when the land was covered with flowers. Happily the daughter Persephone returned to her mother. In her joy at recovering the lost one, Demeter made the corn to sprout in the fields and the earth to bedeck with leaves and blossoms. Straight-away she went to show this happy sight to the princes of Eleusis and moreover she revealed to them her sacred rites and mysteries. So the two Goddesses departed to live happily with the gods of Olympus. (51)

Persephone was also known in ancient Greece as the Kore, the maiden, for her myth is symbol of the child-like innocence that resides in a woman's heart.

The relationship between mother and daughter has a strong impact on the psyche of women, for it is through this natural bondage that the essence of femininity is passed from the previous to the new generation.

The main theme that the poet Homer set forth in this myth is the description of the foundation of the mysteries of Eleusis by the Goddess Demeter. The mysteries consisted in the eternal rejuvenation of plant life. The life of mankind was believed to echo the circular existence – birth, life, death and re-birth – of the vegetation world, for death was regarded as simply a door-step into a new life and each birth was thus celebrated as a come-back of the soul. The existence of the buried seed, represented by Persephone dwelling in the underworld, resting in the earth several months before sprouting, readily suggests a comparison with human destiny and this myth strengthened the hope of agricultural people that for man too the grave was a resting place for a better existence. The poet Homer does not reveal the mystery to the reader for fear of sacrilege, in the same way as a modern Catholic priest performs the ritual of the Eucharist without explaining it for this also represents a mystery of renewal.

The myth of Demeter and Persephone was acted out in the town of Eleusis and it so much represented the intimate faith of the agrarian communities in the secret powers of mother earth that it became the most solemn and famous of religious rites of ancient Greece. The mystery of the Corn Goddess is the mystery of death and the hope of a blissful immortality. For this reason, the ancients regarded initiation in the mysteries of Eleusis as a key to unlock the gates of eternal life.

The Mother Archetype of Demeter

DEMETER, THE GODDESS OF GRAIN, was the most nourishing of all the mother Goddesses. The Romans adopted the myth and re-named Demeter Ceres, from whose name the word cereal is derived. They also re-named Persephone, Proserpina. The most important trait of the Demeter myth is the bondage of the Goddess to her daughter Persephone.

The mother archetype compels women to be caring, to provide nourishment (both physical and psychological), to be generous in their relations to others. This is best exemplified by the myth of Demeter, who finds total fulfillment in her daughter, living her life, in a sense, through Persephone.

Women in whom the Demeter archetype is active have a deeply-rooted need to become mothers. This need may manifest as almost a physical longing to seek completion within themselves through giving birth to a child. Without a child they may feel both physically and psychologically barren, empty, as if a great part of their personality could not find a suitable channel for creative expression. The womb may be seen as the center of a woman's femininity, and it may be that its physical "emptiness" may cause some women to feel psychologically unfulfilled.

The Demeter woman thus seeks in each lover a possible father for her child. She may be, in a sense, not erotically attracted to a man in the way that an Aphrodite woman will, but his personal integrity and desire for a family rank high in her judgment of him. She may see in a man a vehicle for the fulfillment of her desire to become pregnant. In her relationship to men, the Demeter woman is able to maintain herself at a certain distance, for she does not form an erotic and sexual bondage with them. Nor would she ever try to become pregnant in order to keep the man she wants by her side, this she would consider to be a sinful act, her main focus being the child and not a love bondage.

The Demeter woman may feel many affinities with other mothers and she may entertain a deep and intimate friendship with another Demeter woman. She may consider women who do not desire motherhood as not entirely feminine. The pursuit of personal success in a career on the part of a woman may seem to her a derangement of the traditional feminine role which gives the Demeter woman so much security and satisfaction. She may never have fully understood feminism, for she may have felt threatened by the issues raised, interpreting them as undervaluing the role of mother, a role fundamental to her psyche.

The Demeter woman experiences pregnancy and childbirth as an altered state of consciousness. This may represent the peak of satisfaction, happiness and inner fulfillment. During these blissful months, she feels secure for she has the child inside her belly; she knows that after birth the child is going progressively to develop a personality of its own and that it is but the beginning of the end, for the child is bound to leave one day, and this leaving represents a total personal disaster for the Demeter mother. Unlike Isis who is aware that she is but a vehicle for the child's existence, the Demeter woman loves the child from day one with possession. The child is *her own* and the bondage which is created between the two is the most powerful of her life. It would be wrong to think that the Demeter woman is entirely selfish in her love for the little one, for she genuinely feels she can be the one to guide the child through life by opening its wonderful doors. She has eyes for no one but the baby, she may even forget that her husband exists, switching her total attention from him to the new-born. The thread of sexual love that links the Demeter woman to her man may be transformed into maternal love; she may stop seeing him as a lover and treat him as another child, trying to encompass him into her great motherly passion. The child and the running of the home in its function become her sole center of attention.

When the children are old enough to leave home, the Demeter woman feels threatened at her roots. She

seeks to hinder their decision in every possible way, for she fears that without her protection something bad is bound to happen to them. She sees this natural evolution as a great personal calamity which will abruptly end her active function in life. In the myth, Demeter sits sadly under the shade of an olive tree by a well. This can be seen as the psychological position of the Demeter mother after her children leave home. She is seized by a terrible depression and feels as if she was buried into a hole, lacking purpose and sense of direction and she no longer knows how to employ her energies. Her life becomes barren as in the myth she stops the seeds from growing until her daughter Persephone is restored to her. Many Demeter women chose at this point in life to have another child. There may be a considerable age gap between the first child who is by now independent and the last-come, but the Demeter woman feels truly rejuvenated by this new start. This "second" motherhood may be the happy result of a new love or marriage and the Demeter woman feels that life can continue to be as fulfilling as it always was. In this way she can continue to care for the grown-up children without being too possessive of them for she has somebody else to keep her busy.

The Demeter mother may, on the other hand, decide to share her feelings for motherhood within a broader social environment, perhaps by joining a women's group in the active role of family counselor. In this case she will be a great supporter of women who want to form a family, helping them with all the small problems that this decision involves. Or she may work in any other environment where she can take care of others under her protective wing.

Men that seek a mother in a woman are deeply attracted to the Demeter woman, for she fulfills their need, being always present and caring in her practicality and need. She also provides a beautiful and cozy nest for her companion in which he can take refuge from outside events. She may treat her man as if he were a lost child, caring for his laundry, cooking sumptuous dishes and imposing bed-time and rest-hours on him. The result may be a child-like behavior in the man.

Sexuality for the Demeter woman is not an important issue, for she is more cuddly than sexual. Making love is to her a pleasure for it leads to making children; it is not perceived primarily as a source of sexual pleasure. The Demeter woman is thus very faithful to her companion, for she is not at all interested in being with other men in order to discover new things about herself. A man is to be seen as a father and for this function and for the care he provides she is deeply grateful.

The wisdom of old age teaches the Demeter woman the beauty and the blessing of giving birth to a child, nurturing it until adult years and then of the separation with gratitude which grants that the child will seek the support and advice of the mother always.

The rites of Demeter were celebrated at Eleusis when the first grain seed was planted in the earth, for it was the symbol of the activation of the regenerative powers of the Mother Goddess which would grant the continuance of life. The archetype of Demeter becomes activated in a woman when she considers pregnancy and giving birth to a child. This may occur as an impulse when, for instance, a woman sees a close friend with a swelling belly or with a new-born baby. It may also be a desire which stems from the pleasure and satisfaction in the union with a man. The womb may exert an unconscious force to be filled with life, which under particular circumstances the woman may become aware of. The archetype is thus activated by an almost physiological need to seek completion through the conception of a child.

A woman can easily cultivate Demeter by dreaming of the joys of pregnancy and life with children. When children are already present this archetype is strengthened by her feeling maternal toward them, by talking to them on the same plane of understanding and by making herself a participant in their world through finding memories of her own childhood. A child will always respond to a woman who feels like Demeter, for the pull between mother and child is one of the strongest in our psyche and is easily aroused.

Above: The earliest known effigies of a divine figure were those of a female Goddess carved in stone or bone during the Paleolithic period. The mystery of maternity, of the bringing to life of another soul, are here represented by the featureless head of the Goddess and her large abdomen and swollen breasts, symbol of the vessel of life. Right: Persephone represents the unexpressed nature of a woman, immortalized here in rock.

The Daughter Archetype of Persephone

EMETER IS DEPICTED in the Greek myth as a possessive and passionate mother, who finds in her daughter Persephone the only light for her own inner shadows. Persephone leads a trouble-free existence (in the myth we see her picking flowers), is nurtured and cared for solely by her mother within a very tight circle of relationships (the father is never mentioned in the myth). In ancient Greece, Persephone was also known as the Kore, the Maiden, for her archetype represents the child-like innocence in a woman's heart which has not yet been transformed into worldly and sophisticated ways.

Persephone is accustomed to someone else making decisions for her. In the myth, she does not fight Pluto when he abducts her into the Underworld, nor does she take a position when the decision is made on how and where she should spend her life. Persephone has therefore no will to action of her own, for she is always acted upon by the will of others. When this archetype is active in a woman, it endows her with a youthful glow, for she is, in a way, still a child, having led a sheltered existence under the protective wing of the mother, living away from the ordinary world protected by a powerful god-husband. The Persephone woman may appear oddly unwilling to make decisions regarding important issues in her life, such as leaving the parental home, marriage, divorce, taking on a job.

"Elaine" by John A. Grimshaw. The nature of Persephone is perceived on two different levels: on the surface she may seem like a lost sail-boat being swept by the wind hither and thither. On a more profound level, Persephone is master of her journey to the Underworld, she is intimate with the world of shadows and with the forces of darkness that populate our psyche.

These may be cause of concern and worry for anyone else, but the Persephone woman does not seem to care about these worldly and temporal issues, for her focus is on a subterranean current flowing within her which feeds and fulfills her more than any exterior issue could. The mythical figure of Persephone was also perceived in ancient Greece as the guide to the Underworld [52]. This aspect of the Persephone archetype represents that part of the woman's psyche that is in touch with the movements of the unconscious.

The Persephone woman thus exists on two different levels: on the surface she seems without a will of her own, like a lost sail-boat being swept hither and thither by the wind. On a more profound level, she is a complete master of her own destiny for she is able to detect the inner movements of the psyche, which tell her where she is going in her life and what she is doing with herself, regardless of the exterior situation. The Persephone woman values her own nature and gift above everything else, for it is a source of deep fulfillment. Ultimately, no matter what happens to her she is always safe, her child-like innocence and her willingness to follow the deeper, unconscious movements are her anchors in life. But if the Persephone woman had to struggle in order to survive, work long and hard hours in order just to buy enough food to eat, she would no longer be able to function in the same way, for she would then be forced to care more about her exterior actions. In this way, she would corrupt her

own nature in order to survive. This may be why the Persephone woman may generally choose to be cared for, so that she can continue to focus on her inner world. She may marry an older man, who would nurture her perhaps like a father, protect her from the world and let her "pick flowers" within the ring of marriage. Or she may decide never to leave home and her mother, who represents the antithesis to her personality and will always guarantee protection and care.

In her desire to be taken care of the Persephone woman may not fully envisage the consequences that such a decision entails. It may be that too much protection from the world may make her feel cut off from it, which may cause a restlessness of the spirit.

Whether under the influence of a strong mother or of a god-husband, the Persephone woman may find that her own growth is thwarted by their stronger personalities. She is like a small tree struggling to grow in the shadow of a full-grown one. Under such strong influences the Persephone woman may never discover who she really is and may suffer from a suppressed understanding of her sexuality, the center-point of all her energies. In the myth, she is kidnaped by a man, which indicates that she is not able consciously to seduce him nor capable of conducting the kind of relationship which provides nourishment for her own sexuality.

It may be easy to identify the trap into which a Persephone woman may lead herself: in her desire to be protected she may be attracted toward strong personalities, whose influence prevent her from living life to the full. Like a young girl, Persephone thus uses her rich fantasy in order to weave a dream about herself, she auto-hypnotizes herself into believing the impossible, living in another world and seldom "landing" in everyday, "real" life.

In the myth, Zeus decrees that Persephone should live in both worlds within the span of a year. This is the step that Persephone takes in order to find escape from her own strong tendency to be a reflection of her true self. She needs to take part in both the physical, exterior world and in the world of the unconscious. The Persephone woman may be a very good guide to the unconscious of others, for she is able to detect all life's movements easily, as if she were reading an open book. She may be interested in becoming a psychotherapist or a psychologist, bridging thus her understanding of the human psyche with the need to be "grounded" in an interesting profession.

The Persephone woman may therefore find that by giving up some of her fear of the world, she will be greatly rewarded by it. Her understanding of human psychology is a valuable tool both for her rescue of herself and as the linking element with others.

Persephone was worshipped in ancient Greece as the Goddess who helped the descent of the soul to the Underworld from which it would ascend again in a new life. This was celebrated by agrarian communities in winter, when the grain personified by the Goddess and her priestesses "died" within the furrows of the

earth to be born again in spring. Winter was thus a time for introspection, waiting for the forces of nature to change and take on a new course.

The archetype of Persephone is active in a woman when she has ended an important chapter in her life and is waiting for events to open up new possibilities to her. In this "in-between" period she may feel restless for she has not yet found a new direction in her life. She may feel bad about herself for her lack of energy and purpose. However, before any creative act there comes a time when energies, yet unknown for they are not manifest, are welling up within and time cannot be rushed. This is a time when the Persephone archetype can be cultivated by many women, for it gives an invaluable insight into the workings of one's own psyche. A woman may, for instance, learn to analyze her dreams, deriving from them important clues about her life. She may also learn to trust her intuitions about events and people, learning to read in the "signs of destiny" meanings that help her decipher how her relationships and events will develop. The Persephone archetype may never be allowed to surface for it may feel strange and awkward, different as it is from positive action. But the gifts that it brings when it is utilized properly can become a lasting part of a woman's understanding.

The existence of Persephone is divided between the world of light, the physical, exterior world and the world of shadows, the unconscious. In the myth, Zeus decrees that she should spend half of each year with her mother Demeter in the world of the Gods of Olympus and the other half in Hades, with her husband Pluto.

From Mother to Saint –
the Transition between Pagan Worship
and Christian Faith

THE root of the mythology of the mother lies, as we have seen, in the ancient theme developed in Mesopotamia of the Mother Goddess who chooses a lover as the God of fertility. This lover dies periodically in self-sacrifice in order to save his people from famine and death. His body is buried and the god is born again as sprouting grain. The worship of the Great Mother of the Gods and her lover was very popular in the ancient world. Numerous similarities can be drawn between the ancient myths and the Christian tale of the Virgin Mary and Jesus Christ, so much so that the latter could be said to be an inheritance from the myths of the planters. The worship of the Mother of the Gods and her lover became more and more popular under the Roman Empire. Rites and divine honors in their favor were celebrated not only in Rome, but also in other provinces of the Empire such as Spain, Portugal, France, Germany, Bulgaria and Africa. Even while early Christianity took root in Rome, the ancient worship of the God and Goddess of fertility survived it and the two religions were soon competing for allegiance of the West and supremacy in all territories.

There were so many similarities between the two faiths that early Christians were forced into justifying the situation with references to the work of the heathen devil, whereas the pagans accused the Christians of imitating their beliefs and stated that Christ was but a phony Osiris in disguise. Throughout the accounts of the early Christians there is more evidence for striking coincidences between the ancient and the new faith: churches were built on the site of ancient worship; miracles attributed to saints were similar to the acts of semi-gods. The coincidences mark the compromise which the Church had to make in its hour of triumph with the beliefs of the past, which still lingered and were dangerous to an institution whose aim was the winning of souls to the worship of Christ. In fact, the Christian allegory can be read as the last myth of a Mother Goddess and her vegetation God, who bloomed in the desert and separated himself from the earthly domain. [53]

The principal figures of the Goddess and the God of fertility and vegetation are removed from their "worldly" content and sublimated into a spiritual tale that reveals direct messages to our psychological inner world. From the ground we are elevated to the heaven through the Virgin Mary and all the features of this modern myth take on an eternal meaning.

The adoration of the Magii is symbol of the awe and respect we feel at the miracle of birth and their gifts to the Holy Child represents the celebration for the coming of a new life on earth.

175

The Virgin Mary, Mother of God

THE Virgin Mary was the vessel through which the divine manifested itself among men and women, not as symbol, but in flesh and bone. In her unique position, Mary was both the heir of the long tradition of the Mother Goddess and, at the same time, the one who opened the doors to the domain of life eternal.

The Virgin Birth as described by Luke:

In the sixth month the angel Gabriel was sent from God to a city of Galilee named Nazareth, to a virgin betrothed to a man whose name was Joseph, of the house of David; and the virgin's name was Mary. And he came to her and said. "Hail, O favored one, the Lord is with you ! Blessed are you among women!" But she was greatly troubled at the saying, and considered in her mind what sort of greeting this might be. And the angel said to her, "Do not be afraid, Mary, for you have found favor with God. And behold, you will conceive in your womb and bear a son, and you shall call his name Jesus. He will be great, and will be called the Son of the Most High; and the Lord God will give to him the throne of his father David, and he will reign over the house of Jacob for ever; and of his kingdom there will be no end." And Mary said to the angel, "How can this be since I have no husband ?" And the angel said to her, "The Holy Spirit will come upon you, and the power of the most high will overshadow you; therefore the child to be born will be called holy, the Son of God"… And Mary said, "Behold I am the handmaid of the Lord; let it be to me according to your word." And the angel departed from her.

Left: The Virgin and the Child. Mary represents the vessel through which the divine manifested itself in flesh and bone. Right: The archangel Gabriel announces to Mary that she will conceive and give birth to a divine child. The announcement represents the moment in which a woman becomes aware of another life entering her womb.

The extraordinary story of Giovanna, who, alone, dared to challenge the patriarchy of the christian church, in her determination to attain the highest level of spiritual power in order to prove that a woman was not an inferior being.

A bizarre tale, origin of much scandal and shame for the Church, circulated around Europe of the ninth century. A woman allegedly occupied the papal throne legitimately. The legend tells of a woman who dressed as a man and mixed with the high ranks of clerical society, gathering, through her device, knowledge and information on the workings of the church. After years of such preparation, she settled in Rome where she was elected up the steps of the clerical hierarchy, until she was chosen to reign as pope. The fraud is revealed by her giving birth in public during a papal procession. The legend of Joanne, the female pope, grew tall and spread wide, so much so that since then the virility of the elected pope is tested with a marble chair with a hole through which the authenticity of the sex can be proved. On the site of

In 1278 the author Martino Polono writes in his Chronicle of Roman Popes and Emperors *the supposedly true story of Joanne, describing her origin, identity and the time of her holy reign. Martino Polono, however, describes the pseudo-pope as a "he" and the subject of the story as a "she", for she is the prime example of the fickle nature of woman: presumptuous at the beginning, stupid during the act and shameful at the end of it. It is his intention to use Joanne, a woman, to show the illegitimate and sinful act conceived by the female genre. In 1360 Boccaccio dedicates a chapter of his* Illustrious Women *to Joanne, telling her tale of glory and fall into shame. Joanne survives to our own day immortalized in the card of the female pope of the popular Visconti Tarot cards as symbol of female wisdom and intuition.*

the unholy birth, there stands a statue representing the female pope and her child and still nowadays the popes impose a deviation on the course of public processions in order to avoid the shameful spot. This very rule reveals the truth of the story of Joanne which has been denied by the Church itself throughout the centuries.

The history of the Christian Church has been formed, over the centuries, partly by legend and partly by truth. The existence of legendary characters such as Joanne, the female pope, can never be formally attested, but nevertheless has had a great impact upon the popular mind and her tale has been told again and again for centuries.

The representative of the powers of the Goddess on earth was woman. In her function of priestess, of guardian of the mysteries of the feminine, woman became a sacred prostitute for through love-making she brought the power of the Goddess to the human sphere. Whether in public celebration or in the privacy of her temple chamber, the sacred prostitute expressed her true feminine nature. Her beauty and sensuous body were not used in order to gain security, power or possessions. Her raison d'etre was to worship the Goddess through love-making, the laws of her feminine nature were harmonious with those of the divinity. When the time came in which the Goddess was no longer worshipped, the physical and spiritual aspects of the feminine were declared evil. Societies which had been matriarchal in focus, where agriculture and religion were the primary concerns of life, became patriarchal, led by men for whom commerce, expansion and war were the channels for creativity and for a new psychological imprint which preferred to risk life rather than produce it. Change in cultural and social values determined a profound change in religious attitude : man created a male God in his image and established a new doctrine which reflected his beliefs in male supremacy. The Goddess' temples dedicated to love and life were substituted by temples where mankind prepared itself for death and life eternal. Love and sexuality were separated from the body in order to attain spiritual life. Mary, stripped of all her womanly connotations, became the holy vessel for the holy birth, an ideal all women had to incarnate. Mary may be adored but not worshipped, lest she should become a channel through which the worship of the Goddess may be re-established. The ancient Goddess was replaced by the institution of the Mother Church, an organization took the place of warmth and relationships between the sexes. Mary incarnated the encompassing ideal, containing in her holiness her child Christ the Savior, whom she begot by immaculate conception, the clerical corpus, formed by men stripped of their virility, and the people, whose spirit was separate from the physical forces that governed them.

This extract from the life of Mary, represents a mythical inheritance from the motifs of ancient mythology. As it has been described in the chapter dedicated to the archetype of the virgin, the term "virgin" was synonymous in the ancient world with "maid" or unmarried woman. It was not unusual to find women who took lovers and even conceived children outside wedlock, if marriage did not suit their life-style.

This situation was not subject to moral judgment as it would perhaps be in our modern world, where the misunderstanding of the term by Christian ecclesiasts causes so much degrading harassment for women of the faith. Children born from the temple women were called by the Semites "virgin-born," because their mothers were not married. [54] Mary's impregnation by the spirit of God is not unusual if compared with the

birth of other mythical children. The relationship between man and gods was a close and intimate affair and the notion that women were impregnated by gods or spirits seemed to be a matter of commonly accepted knowledge. Gabriel means literally "divine husband." Zeus, the father of the Greek pantheon, was believed to have been virgin-born. Plato was the virgin-born son of the sun God. Impregnation by a god or spirit was the acceptable explanation for pregnancy in most pagan countries where the sexual act was part of the fertility rites.

"Witches Sabbath" by Goya. Contrary to most artistic depictions, the medieval witches actually unearthed the lost wisdom of the matriarchal age. The feminine essence is the principle of restoration of all life and was applied to medicine and mystical experiences.

The belief that Jesus was born from the physically virgin body of Mary has been maintained to this day by the Church Fathers; the legend was promoted to ennoble women, for it was believed to elevate their humanity onto the spiritual level. This has causedcenturies of disruption and disorientation in the psyche of both men and women so that still today we are trying to recover from it. As Christianity became more and more widespread, its dogmas became

more forcefully promoted in order to eradicate pagan worship and the relation to woman was expressed in the collective worship of Mary, a figure stripped of all humanity. The image of woman thus lost its value in the eyes of men and women. The virgin birth was an impossible ideal to which followers of the religion sought to attain; women's spiritual goal was to become like Mary, pure and untouched, and motherhood became a saintly ordeal from which a woman could on no grounds be distracted by sexual desires. Men repressed the natural sexual instinct, for it was sinful to desire carnal pleasures; the sexual instinct had been displaced from its natural and only pattern and the repression created an unconscious force which was projected on external objects.

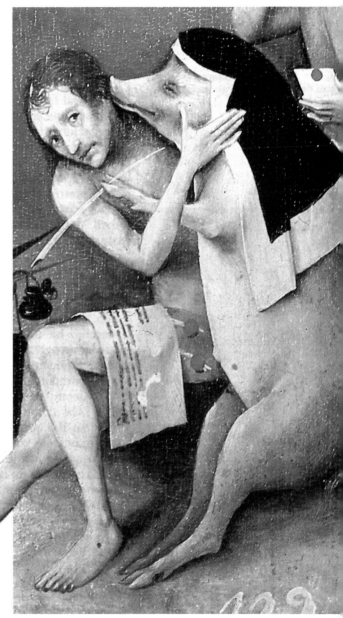

Left: The identification of woman with Eve, the harlot and temptress, on the one hand and with Mary, the holy vessel, on the other became so natural in Christian thought that generations of men and women lived and died unable to place their natural instincts within this dogmatic context. Right: Sexual repression promoted by the church created an unconscious force which took the form of female demonic features. Women's existence was a reminder of sinful physical desires, which had to be resisted through fear of eternal punishment.

The devaluation of woman was, so to speak, compensated by her endowment of demonic traits.[55] In other words, if woman was to be a saint, any unsaintly female representative of true femininity which tempted men away from becoming holy and pure in their turn was regarded as a demon. The consequence of the repression of natural instincts was the witch hunt, an abominable and indelible blot on the Middle Ages. But this, unfortunately, was not the only consequence; the splitting off of the ancient Mother Goddess, who combined maternity and sexuality, and of whom Mary was a descendent, into a harlot and temptress on the one hand, and into a female ascetic on the other, created a general activation of the unconscious in each individual. Unable to place their natural way of life within this destructive Christian dogmatic context, men and women resorted to fanaticism. The horror of the Inquisition was nothing more than the terrible doubt that evil was lurking everywhere, in black cats, in chickens, at night, under the skirts of beautiful women, in the cells of priests, in the eyes of monks. It was perhaps not evil, but nature that was forcing its way through all these layers of repression and fanaticism, most of which still exist today. It is a popular belief nowadays that the more we suppress the more we desire, especially so with that which is "evil."

"The Temptation of St. Anthony" by D. Morello. Woman was tempted by the forces of evil and in turn she tempted man. The greatest virtue was to overcome the pleasures of the flesh, subduing desire by fasting, self-castigation and personal deprivation of all kinds.

The Archetype of Mary

T HE ARCHETYPE OF THE Virgin Mary works in a woman when she experiences pregnancy and childbirth as a spiritual experience. She awaits the birth of the "little one" as she would await a miracle and a deep sense of peace fills her, noticed by all around her.

Ancient Hindu wisdom teaches that the law of the three states Tamas, Raja and Sattva – is the natural law of life and all things develop according to its parameters. This law can be best explained by applying it to the element of water: Tamas, the first state, in this case represents ice. Tamas is the state of matter, of concreteness. The second stage, Raja, remains matter, but it is inhabited by a soul with awareness of itself. In our case it corresponds to water itself – its fluidity is in perpetual transformation, an incessant becoming which represents life. The third stage, Sattva, is the sublimation of the spirit which inhabits matter, transcends the heaviness and becomes light and free. In the example of water it represents vapor, an essence which cannot be contained. It represents the spirituality of matter, the esprit of creativity.

Frédérick Leboyer, the eminent French doctor who revolutionized Western birthing methods, has applied this law to pregnancy and childbirth in his book *Le Sacre de la Naissance*. [56] In his view, the mother who is really aware of the spirit of the child and brings her total consciousness to light during birth is a woman who enters the Sattva state at this moment in life. In our own Western terms, this state is reached when the Virgin Mary archetype is active, for the act of creation is an act of the soul as well as of the body.

Many women with the qualities of Mary are able to tell when the soul of the child enters the body remaining deeply in tune with the child's feelings and movements. In the myth the archangel Gabriel announces the imminent incarnation of the child Jesus in the womb of Mary, a metaphor perhaps for the child's soul making itself manifest to the mother through a dream or a vision. Many women can often tell after intercourse that they are pregnant and the medical examination which follows the missed onset of menstruation always proves their intuition right.

In order to preserve the purity of the baby's psyche and perceptions, the mother may seek revolutionary birthing methods, which respect the natural way of birth. Birth then becomes a holy experience, perhaps performed in candle light, with soft music playing. Indian women belonging to the Brahmin cast give birth in such a way, training their breath with chanting and maintaining the body supple with yogic asanas, for theirs is the cast closest to spiritual elevation and everything has to be done to maintain the purity of the child intact. Gautam Buddha is said to have had a princely birth and led a princely life – thus bringing him to enlightenment. It is now clinically proven that babies born at home, when the mother is healthy and

there are no complications, in a soft and happy environment, seem very different in their approach to life to children born under mechanical hospital conditions. They are evidently more trusting, more in tune with nature and with others.

Women have a birthright to procreate in the most beautiful way, breaking thus the curse that patriarchy set on them. For out of woman comes the future of mankind.

"Immaculate Conception" by Giovannibattista Tiepolo (1696-1770).

CHAPTER SIX

Priestess and Wise Woman

The Guardians of the Mysteries – The Sacred fire of Vesta – The Archetype of
Vesta – The Priestesses of the Moon – The Archetype of the Priestess –
The Holy Grail

The Guardians of the Mysteries

HE ESSENCE OF WOMAN lends itself, easily and naturally, to the role of priestess, of guardian and invoker of the great mysteries of the unknown.

Woman contains all the opposing forces, which, when observed in nature or in the animal kingdom, leave us breathless. We have seen, in previous chapters, the contrasting mechanisms at work in woman. In our examination of the myths we saw that the Goddess that is woman could be Kali, the creator and destroyer, Isis, the mother of all, Aphrodite, in her power to be eternally in love, Circe and Medea, in their enticing games of love magic and sorcerous entrapments. Just as the Goddess is found in many forms, woman is likewise multifaceted, changing constantly as in the impetuous current of a spring flood. The blood in her veins throbs in unison with the natural forces. She is therefore the perfect medium to express the forces at work in the conscious and unconscious of humanity and existence. Her natural intimacy with her instinctual self finds a channel of expression through the body; in birth, in menstruation, in sexuality and in motherhood. The mystical aspect of the self finds expression in rituals, in the enclaves of priestesses and in magic. The female essence is, as it were, a fluid which bridges the gap between the plane of reality on which we live our conscious lives each day, and that other unknown domain, not easily explained, that nevertheless lives in us all.

Today there are no priestesses, no mysteries in which a whole culture believes, none that we can join together as a complete force to fulfill as in ancient times. Society is composed of individuals, living together with common *material* interests. The intimate

domain of the self remains unaided within the modern social frame, and therefore it is often disregarded.

The following myths – tales of priestesses, each guarding a mystery of human life – may be far away from us in time, but still they hold timeless values. The myths were created to inspire, then as now, for whomever came within their sphere, an essence and a reminder of the sacredness of existence.

Temple of Holy Prostitution, Laksamana, India

The Sacred Fire of Vesta

THE Goddess Vesta was Rome's protectress of the hearth. Within her sacred temple burned a pure flame attended at all times by six highly revered women, the Vestal Virgins. The fire was extinguished at the end of each year and relit in the primitive style, by rubbing together two sticks from an oak tree. The dress of the Vestal Virgin resembled a Roman bridal gown. On assuming her vow, the dedicated acolyte was solemnly clasped by the Pontifex Maximus, the chief priest of the city, who spoke the words: *Te, Amata, capio!* "My Beloved, I take possession of thee!," and was symbolically married, through the Pontifex, to the phallic deity of the Palladium. If she broke her vow of chastity, she was buried alive. [57]

The tradition of the Vestal Fire, which had been kept burning for more than six hundred years in Rome, until it was put out and the ritual erased by the Christians, finds its roots far and away, at the dawn of the first civilizations. Vesta was the oldest Goddess-Matriarch of Rome and her figure represented the focal point among all the Latin Gods and Goddesses. Her temple was to the imperial city what the hearth was to the Roman, and indeed the modern, household. As long as the flame was alive, any man or woman inhabiting the city felt secure in his or her position within a social and religious environment.

The main symbols of the Sacred Fire of Vesta are the female divinity of Vesta herself, the virgin priestesses and the roundness of her temple containing fire within.

Vesta was the Roman version of the Greek Goddess Hestia. Her name means literally "hearth" and she represented the home place, every man's center. The hearth of Hestia and Vesta was, thus, to each member of the household, an "ombilicum orbis" or the navel of the earth, the (h)earth being another form of the earth.

The round temple of Vesta was the city's hearth. The shape must have been a reminder of the womb, the creative center of a woman's body. The earth was also believed to be a mother, and within her womb, animals and trees were created. Human life had always been seen as a microcosm of the greater realm of animal, plant and divine life.

In order to grasp the meaning of the perpetual fire of Vesta, we must return to the Mesopotamic myth of the Mother Goddess, whose lover, the fertility Corn God, was sacrificed yearly for the growth of the grain and crops. In certain rituals, the Corn King was killed in the field, for the running of his blood was believed to fertilize the earth, his remains then burned and the ashes thrown on the furrows. On some occasions, the god of vegetation was represented by a man dressed as an oak tree (the tree sacred to the Goddess), who was also burned. This myth and its rituals were adopted by many other cultures that developed after the Meso-

---

The office of the Vestal Virgins in the Goddess's temple in ancient Rome consisted in guarding a pure flame which was extinguished once a year and relit in the primitive style, by rubbing two sticks of oak wood together. The flame represented the spirit of the Goddess, protectress of the Roman hearth.

potamic civilizations. The myth survived, modified by the passing of time and different linguistic, religious and social customs, and was observed in Imperial Rome under the ritual of the Vestal Fire. Vesta was thus the inheritor of the great Mother Goddess, and her priestesses, virgins for they were not married, carried out her function of maintenance of life.

The fire which had burnt the God of fertility in ancient times, came to represent the flame of existence which was always burning within the womb/temple of the Goddess. The fire was extinguished at the end of each year, a memory of the God of fertility journeying to the underworld in winter to resurrect again with the first wheat sprouts. The Virgin was symbolically united with the male deity by the chief priest of Rome, a ritual observed even in Mesopotamia, to symbolize the Goddess choosing a lover, and through their union, granting the growth and fertility of crops. After the symbolic marriage, the fire was rekindled.

The temple of Vesta in Rome was said to be white, the same color as the ashes that woman first gathered, perhaps as far back as Neolithic times, after the fire had died down in the primitive hearth. The color white survived in the bridal gowns of the Vestal Virgins, for it was a symbol of the hearth, the womb, the center of life and the fire that fed it. To this day, brides are dressed in white, to represent purity and unspotted virginity. Virginity was the quality of the priestess of Vesta upon whom the continuance of life was placed. The Christian Pope, his name deriving from the Latin term of address for the chief priest, *Pontifex*, and his representatives still unite the bride to the man – himself the lost symbol of the male fertility God. The modern marriage ceremony is thus a seal on the procreation of life. We can see these modern "rituals" as yet more evidence of our distant past, carried forward through the ages. Rituals which we still observe, even though we have lost the full context of their origin.

Left: The round temple of Vesta in ancient Rome represented the city's hearth. The shape was a reminder of the womb, the creative center in a woman's body. Vesta means literally hearth, the home place and center of origin of mankind. The temple stood between the microcosm of human life and the greater realm of animal, plant and divine life.

The Archetype of Vesta

HE ARCHETYPE OF Vesta represents woman's inner wisdom. Like a priestess, the Vesta woman takes each event in her life, each circumstance, as a spiritual lesson through which she can learn to transcend the world. The Vesta woman may thus appear to other "mortals" as not totally human, as detached from reality, never taking a stand on issues of human importance. She is always well disposed toward others, never thinking anything bad, never gossiping, almost like a saint.

She filters through her mind all issues that may hurt her and transforms them into positive growth patterns. Her nature may cause some problems in her relationship toward others, especially women. She seems unreal, as if she was repressing her deeper feelings in order to promote a holy image of herself to the world. Her ego has not dissolved as she may want others to believe, but it exists firmly in the negation of the self. She may be the kind of woman who congratulates herself on *not reacting* when an issue either hurts her or makes her happy, for this is a proof that she is beyond human imperfection and is not swayed by anything, being totally centered upon her path.

Her warmth toward men borders on the impersonal, which may give them the impression that she is a free woman, giving them plenty of room in the relationship to do whatever they wish. She may appear not to mind if her man goes with another woman, for this is yet another lesson to be learnt on detachment, even though she may cry her heart out by herself. This is the kind of issue which enrages other women, for they may feel she is negating her true feelings, being somewhat dishonest with her loved one by giving him a false impression, and additionally of course, other women are able to detect the loneliness and sadness caused by this self-imposed role.

One of the main issues of the Vesta woman is her loneliness, which incidentally she values highly, for she is truly different from others in her approach to life, as she genuinely can take refuge and revitalize herself in quiet moments. Her wisdom also stems from her ability to ponder upon events and understand their deeper meaning. However, the Vesta woman may be so focused on her inner life that she may forget about her worldly self, creating damage to her own psyche. The Vesta woman, for instance, treats her own house like a temple. She keeps it clean and bedecked with flowers, as if she were honoring a deity through household work. The disruption that others create often negates her efforts, making her feel futile and unrespected by others. However, she has no heart to tell them about her hurt feelings, for she is set on understanding their needs even more than her own.

The true wisdom of the archetype is revealed when the Vesta woman acknowledges her humanity and finds the courage to be wholly open about her feelings, sharing with others her loneliness, sadness, happiness and

even her bad temper. When a Vesta woman can do this, she becomes most trusting and trustworthy, for she is revealing her true self to the world. Life may then become a spiritual experience, for she will feel greatly enriched by the psychological change of focus. Her warmth will be genuine, her love great. She will become "rounded" like the hearth that represents the Goddess, leaving all "edges" of her character behind.

By being in the world, she will not diminish her spiritual endowment, which may be one of the fears that prevent her from changing, but actually increase it. Like a mathematical formula, inner richness lights the flame of the heart and extinguishes the ego, in the same proportion as disciplined self-denial feeds the ego-mind.

Her relationship with women will be greatly improved for she is a formidable friend and companion, always finding a good word in times of need. She will represent for everyone who loves her a hearth, a stable reference point. In her relationship with men, she will become the woman she really is, able to feel passion consuming her heart. She is an inventive and warm lover as well as a good friend and counselor, making the best of mates for a man.

Vesta was not popularly known through myths and representations, but rather through rituals which were performed in her honor in the private and public houses of ancient Rome. The kindling of the hearth was, for instance, a daily ritual performed by women of different social strata which granted the beneficial presence of the Goddess within a home. The powers of Vesta were thus called to protect the dwelling and its inhabitants from the influence of evil. Sitting together around the hearth was a common ritual performed by Roman families which were bonded together by the pervading power of the fire and of the home.

The Vesta archetype can be activated by doing quiet, unhurried household work. Even the most outgoing woman finds that there are times when cleaning, placing flowers in a vase, ironing and folding away clean laundry in lavender-scented drawers, doing needle-work on a cushion-cover, are sources of great relaxation and excellent activities to find oneself again. Caring for one's own home as a ritual to Vesta may invest one with calm and gratefulness, as if one was really cleaning one's spirit from alien influences, thus bringing focus upon oneself and peace of mind.

The Priestesses of the Moon

T HE ancients regarded their inner experiences as the meter with which to measure the phenomena of the outside world. The observation of the workings of nature left a deep impression and the phenomena were recorded on rock or stone, to remind them of the psychic impact that had been felt. Thus the sun, the stars, the waters, the sky, the earth, the trees, the animals, all were depicted and recorded, in order to recollect their memory, as if by magic. Today, we still relate our dreams, looking for meaning in the events experienced during sleep. The symbols used to describe the experiences have not changed throughout the history of human consciousness for we need simple and yet all-containing vehicles to encompass these archetypal images.

Among such symbols stands the Moon. It exercises power over the waters, over vegetation, illuminating with reflected light the darkness of the night sky. It is accompanied by a myriad of stars at every appearance, changing in cycles from sickle-shaped to full moon, to black moon, like woman, the Goddess of the ancients. For all its qualities it was conceived of as a deity, and Goddess and moon were one and inseparable, as if the moon was the physical appearance of the Goddess in the world of man.

Temples dedicated to the many important Goddesses of the ancient world, always had the moon as the primary symbol of the divinity. An entourage of women served as priestesses in the temple, in charge of the magical practices intended to foster the fertilizing power of their symbol. The cycles were strictly observed and specific rituals performed for each lunar phase. The priestess's most important function was the care of the water supply, the making of rain and the magical control of the weather. The moon was in fact believed to influence not only the ebbs and flows of rivers, seas and all other water courses, but also the movement of rain clouds and the changes of the weather. Water was of fundamental importance to the agricultural communities, for it made the ground fertile. The association of ideas in the ancient mind saw the moon's cycle as synonymous with the monthly cycle of the woman. The moon was therefore responsible for the fertility of women and the bringing of babies into the world. And, as the earth was the Great Mother, so the moon with its power over the waters, was held responsible for the fertility of the land.

Rituals for rain-making are still performed today by tribes living in Africa and South America. The moon priestesses first clean out water springs and wells, and then draw fresh water and throw it over their bodies, often also throwing fetishes in the water. This latter custom has survived to this day even in civilized Rome: it is said that anyone visiting the Fontana di Trevi, built over one of the many springs that used to provide the city's supply of water, should throw in a coin to bring luck and plenty. The coins, round in shape like the full moon when it draws the tides to their maximum swelling, are the modern fetishes of richness. [58]

Fertility was not regarded as a quality inherent in the biological nature of woman. It was considered a gift from the Goddess and it was believed that the moon

could strongly influence this gift. The part that men played in the begetting of a child was unclear, for all natural phenomena were attributed to the will of the divinity. In a world devastated by incurable sickness, war and constant invasions from barbaric tribes, the maintenance of a healthy young population was fundamental to the survival of the civilization. Thus, the rituals performed by the moon priestesses to foster the fertility of the land and of women were held sacred. The will of the Goddess found a channel of expression in the physical world.

Upon entering service in the temple, girls underwent an initiation to the mysteries of the Goddess: they sacrificed their virginity and entered a *hieros gamos*, or sacred marriage, which was consummated with the priest, as representative of the fertility god, lover of the Goddess, or by a stranger visiting the temple. It seems to have been quite common that the temple priestesses played the role of sacred prostitutes. Much of their lives was thus dedicated to the fostering of fertility. In fact, ordinary women as well as the queens of the land had to undergo a similar experience within the temple, giving themselves to the will of the Goddess and making love with ordinary men in order to ensure richness. The mating of the God and Goddess, or their representatives, was deemed essential to the propagation of plants and animals. The union of the divine couple was simulated and multiplied on earth by the real, though temporary, union of the human sexes, to ensure the fruitfulness of the ground, of the animals and of men and women alike. [59]

The *hieros gamos* reflects an important custom and belief of the ancient world. In Rome, for instance, the King owed his pre-eminence to the fact that he was,

Left: "The Hands" by Edward Munch. Above: Upon entering service in a temple, young girls underwent a ceremony of initiation into the mysteries. They sacrificed their virginity and entered a hieros gamos, *or sacred marriage, with the priest, a representative of the ancient god of fertility. The fostering of fertility was a duty of each priestess in the service of the Goddess.*

symbolically, married to a Vestal virgin. This was the inheritance of the old tradition of the Great Goddess of the Mesopotamic countries, who took a lover in order to promote fertility. The enactment of the tradition implied that the queen took a lover, who became a sort of functional king, in order to fulfill the Goddess's wishes. With the passing of time, the tradition was changed by the arrival of patriarchy. Nevertheless, private property and the lineage of the great kings was passed on from generation to generation through the blood-line of the mother, for a long time in such countries as ancient Greece and Rome, before this custom was eradicated.

From paintings and decorations on temple walls and ritual vases, it seems that the ritual of fertility involved the partaking of sacred food. The communion meal of barley cakes or any other cereal, symbolized the partaking of the body of the god, lover of the Goddess. The wine drunk was symbol of his blood, which was drawn at his death in order to fertilize the fields. The same symbolism is still maintained in the Christian ritual. The wine may have also been an intoxicating drink, called "soma," or the "drink of the gods." A vessel divided into several parts and each containing a few seeds of the grain cultivated in the area, with a lighted candle in the center, was carried by a priestess. The candle was symbol of the "flame of life," the fertilizing power and light produced by the union of the female and male principles. The vessel was called *kernos*, which represented the womb of the Great

LACIA †SCAEVFIMIA

Mother, giver of life, and was often used to symbolize the Goddess herself. [60]

The "mysteries" entered by the priestesses through rituals, were the seeking for a relation between man and god. The ritual was a channel, a bridge that linked the temporal, unenlightened human plane with the divine. The symbols, such as the flame, grain seeds and corn cakes, served as a "language" of intimate communication with the deity. In later ages, the witches developed spells to bridge the gap between the known and the unknown. Today we analyze certain symbols in our dreams in order to understand the subtler folds of our being. The search for the "inner flame," for the divine substance within, is not, as one might suspect, the modern trend resulting from an age of disillusion. It has always belonged to the heart of man. Indeed, sages and masters of all ages, since primordial times, have sought to communicate their ecstatic experiences to others. And because the experience is particular, not perceived through the unenlightened senses, then a special language must be used to convey it. This language is made up of painted or written symbols. The holy scriptures of all religions are deeply impregnated in symbology and the primary function of the priest is, hopefully, that of "translator" of the symbols into a comprehensible, ordinary language.

Symbols are thus very important, for they remain impressed upon our consciousness. They not only convey the experience, but they serve as guidelines to the person who has embarked upon the "pathless

Above: "The Holy Supper" by Leonardo da Vinci. An important ritual in the worship of the divinity involved the consummation of sacred food, for it symbolized the partaking of the body of the God, lover of the Goddess. The wine drunk was symbol of his blood, which was drawn at his death in order to fertilize the land. This symbology has been maintained to our own day in the sacred Christian ritual of the communion. Right: "Madonna and Child" by Leonardo da Vinci. The figure of the Madonna is the idealization of the process of pregnancy and birth: the woman has received the divine substance within her and has given birth to it. Woman represents the perfect channel for the manifestation of the divine in bone and flesh.

path." As in the popular children's tale of Tom Thumb, in which the little boy leaves behind a track of millet seeds when he enters, on his own, the dark and dangerous woods, so the visionary leaves behind symbols, like seeds, for the one that will come after him. Mythology and its symbology is the language of an enlightened experience, which anyone can understand. [61]

The function of the priestess differs greatly from that of the priest. Whereas he is a "translator" of sym-bols, she is a conveyer. The capacity of woman to "receive" in order to "give" makes her the perfect channel for the divine. The figure of the Madonna is, for instance, the idealization of the process of pregnancy and birth: the woman has received into her the divine substance, the purity of the child, and has given birth to it. The "channel" does not own the experience, it simply conveys it, in a continuum of receiving and giving, giving and receiving.

The Archetype of the Priestess

HIS ARCHETYPE IS AGAIN being expressed by women after centuries of spiritual denial imposed by patriarchy. For a long time, women were literally cut off from the spiritual path in the Western world, for they were considered only surrogate human beings, inferior to men who were the only ones capable of enlightenement. Today, East and West are bridging the gap that kept them separate and a different perception of spirituality is slowly entering the Western mind. The archetype becomes active when a woman chooses to follow a guru and allows him or her to open her eyes to the mysteries of the inner path. Meditation and a different meaning of life is very important to woman, for she has been locked for centuries in the role of wife and mother. A rainbow is available now to her and she is finally free to chose any colour, any role, any archetype she feels most drawn toward.

Right: "La Dama de Elche", Prado, Madrid. In ancient times the essence of aristocracy was its link with the world of gods who ruled on earth through kings and queens. The maintenance of the divine will was a royal duty and the royal house was, foremost, the house of the supreme priest and priestess.

The Holy Grail

THE office of the priestesses of the Moon entailed tasks other than representing the Goddess in her life-giving power. Among these was the "honor of death," the administering of her dark and terrible aspect through death. Sacrifices of men, animals and small children were perpetrated in her honor, as the remains of skeletons found in ancient temples prove. The chief priestess of the Celtic tradition, for instance, was required to serve as chief executioner in certain sacrifices. The heads of the captured soldiers after a war were severed and the blood was drained into a cauldron or special vessel. The container of the sacrificial blood was called the Cauldron of Regeneration, for the blood poured into it was thought to possess regenerative powers. Death in the ancients' mind was never purposeless, for the belief in afterlife and regeneration in human life as well as in the plants was strongly rooted. The fumes exuded from the boiling of the sacrificial brew were intoxicating and the "inspiring" of the fumes sent priests and priestesses into a maddening frenzy. This was the original source of inspiration for the early poets. To take in the source of sacrifice in honor of the Goddess was to imbibe oneself with her divine substance. The poem that resulted from this religious process was thus believed to have been "divinely inspired". [62]

Left: The office of the priestesses of the Moon entailed the representation of the Goddess in her terrible aspect of Lady of Death. Sacrifices of animals, small children and men in her honor were performed as rituals and the remains placed within the walls of the temple. Right: Morgan Le Fay drew her power from the Cauldron of Regeneration, which in Celtic lore and myth was the vessel into which the sacrificial blood was poured for it was thought to possess regenerative powers.

Right: The chalice which received the sacrificial blood was protected by powerful spells and incantations, cast with the power of magic known by mankind a long time ago. The vessel represented the cyclic nature of all existence and the seeking of man for his own soul through the understanding of the mysteries of the Goddess.

The Celtic Cauldron, roundly shaped like the womb of the Goddess, was the source of the legendary Holy Grail of the Arthurian epics. The Holy Grail is a mystery which still today has not been unveiled completely. It is shrouded in symbolism and powerful magic, as it was performed in ancient times, something we have completely forgotten now. It is said to be protected by spells, cast by magicians a long time ago. The Grail is believed to be the Chalice in which the Holy Blood of God was poured upon his death. The power of this symbol lies in the fact that the holy blood is believed to possess the regenerative power of Christ the Savior. Whenever it is mentioned in the legends it is associated with a King, who is either dead or mortally ill. His country reflects his poor condition, for it is barren and sick, like a wasteland. The task of the knights, the men of honor surrounding the King, is to retrieve the Holy Grail and bring it back to the King and his country in order to "save" them. To drink from the Chalice bestows regeneration, just as it did, in ancient times, to partake of the blood of the King, the lover of the Goddess, who had been sacrificed. The King of the Celtic legend is neither dead nor alive, but is suspended in a half-state between life and death, until the mystery of the Grail is revealed to a mortal man, who has achieved the illumination through his courage and endurance. Finding the Grail is thus a holy quest, symbol of finding our own light, which illuminates our consciousness, redeeming us from the eternal cycle of birth, life and death and transporting us into the eternal, blessed light.

The mystery of the vessel is the mystery of the Goddess: she incarnates the very principle, reflected in woman and in all humans therefore, of eternal life. Her power is of a regenerative kind, she is the one to break the spell of the cyclic wheel all humans are bound to. The worship of the Goddess was a symbol of the seeking of man for the essence of his own soul. Her myth is therefore eternal, for it is deeply and instinctively linked to the destiny of mankind. It is only through the realization of the feminine power to receive and yield, again, and again, that mankind will attain the final liberation.

CHAPTER SEVEN

Muse and Inspirer

The Triple Goddess – Believing the Impossible Woman –
The Archetype of the Muse

The Triple Goddess

T WAS IN THE POETIC language of ancient Europe that the Goddess became the inspirer and Muse of poets and bards. Many myths and symbols of the Western cultural tradition of poetic lore, inspired by the Muse, had been developed in the Mesopotamic countries. Many of the stories, however, became confused with the passage of time and the frequent modifications of different cultures and beliefs. The myths were shaped anew according to the various religious, social and linguistic changes, from country to country and era to era. [63]

But there are a few fundamental symbols that remained pure. Among them, the most remarkable is perhaps the symbol of the Triple Goddess:

"Diana in the leaves green,
Luna that so bright does sheen,
Persephone in Hell."
(Skelton, *Gardland of Laurel*)

The divinity in her triple aspect represents the Goddess of the Sky, of the Earth and of the Underworld. As Goddess of the Sky, she was the Moon: the New Moon is the Goddess as a girl, the Full Moon is the Goddess as a woman and the waning Moon is the Goddess as a wise old woman. As Goddess of the Earth she animated all trees, plants and animals. She ruled the three Seasons: spring, summer and winter. As Goddess of the Underworld, she was concerned with Birth, Procreation and Death.

The triple Goddess was adopted as the Muse by

Left: " O! how I dreamt of things impossible," declared William Blake. The myth is the public dream of things impossible, while the dream is the private myth which tells of things impossible.

the poets of ancient Europe. Foremost, her three aspects formed almost a magic circle of beginning (birth), development (life) and end (death), which suited the poetic theme most favorably, for poems were sung to a captive audience and not read privately as they are today. Moreover, the triple Muse was seen as woman in her divine character – she was the poet's enchantress, his only theme.

The Muse was thus named the Triple Muse, or Ninefold Muse and in the Celtic countries of Wales and Ireland, where the poetic lore developed to its highest level, she was given the name Cerridwen.

Cerridwen's name was derived from the Spanish word "cerda," meaning sow. The town of Puigcerda (*Puig*, hill and *Cerda*, sow, in Catalan), in the Spanish Pyrenees, was dedicated in ancient times to the Goddess of life and death and still nowadays the killing of the pig in winter is a sacred festivity. The myth was carried by sea to the Celtic countries and Cerridwen was believed to take the shape of a sow. She is said to have presided over a magic caul-

Above: The triple Goddess represented the inspiring Muse for the poets of ancient pagan Europe whose nature suited the poetic theme. Right: The alluring character of the Muse could take the human form of a genteel damsel and bewitch men into the reign of oblivion.

dron; the poet inhaled or "inspired" the magic fumes and became enchanted and, in his frenzy, wrote his soul's dedications to the Muse. The Welsh bards were called "cerdorrion," sons of Cerridwen and Taliesin. The wizard Merlin of the Arthurian legend was their leader. The Christian bards took the Virgin Mary as their cauldron of inspiration, for she was symbol of the "vessel" of life.

Brigit was another triple Muse reigning in the Empire of Brigantia, which included parts of Spain and France, and the British Isles. The Christians found her cult difficult to eradicate and proclaimed her saint. Bridewell, the female prison in London, was originally one of her nunneries. As well as being an inspiring muse for Welsh and Irish bards, spells and incantations were chanted in her honor at springs and holy wells, for she was believed to cure all ills.

*"Three Ladies came from the East,
One with fire and two with frost,
Out with thee, fire, and in with thee, frost."*

This was an incantation against burns – the user was to dip nine bramble leaves in spring water and apply them to the scald. The charm had to be said three times for each leaf for the cure to be effective. [64]

The poetic tradition of ancient Europe was based on magical principles in which the Goddess as Muse played a most important role, and her symbols served the purpose of parameters for the development of a theme. The tradition of the Celtic bards who went from village to village and recited under a tree or by the chimney of the greatest house was the main force that kept the mythology that had been developed in the early civilizations alive by word of mouth. In England, for instance, social life was based on important dates of the agricultural calendar, which were celebrated as festivals. Candlemas, May Day, Midsummer Day, Lammas, Michaelmas, Halloween and Christmas were the days in which people made merry and poetry was declared.

Each bard developed his story around a Theme, which was fixed. The Theme was an ancient story of the birth, life, death and resurrection of the god of the Waxing Year. The central chapters of the story concerned the god losing the battle with the god of the Waning Year, for love of the beautiful and capricious Threefold Goddess, their mother, lover and bringer of death. The poet identified himself with the god of the Waxing Year and the Muse was the Goddess; the god of the Waning Year was a symbol for the poet's other self, his double, who, when encountered, provoked instant death. The god of the Waning Year represented, in psychological terms, the Self. [65]

The Goddess was portrayed as a lovely looking young woman, pale-faced, with red lips, startling blue

eyes and long, fair hair. Her becoming appearance, however, disguised her power of transformation. She could become sow, mare, bitch, vixen and many other female animals. She could transform herself in a full-moon night's breeze and make the wolves howl in recognition. Whenever she appeared in one of her disguises, a shiver would run down a man's spine, tears would well up in his eyes and he would be seized by a cold, inexplicable terror. She was the inspirer of all things dark and unknown, spiriting men in her misty domain, from which they would never return. The Goddess haunts the poet and the sensitive man, delving into his most intimate thoughts and corners of his soul, until, enchanted by her spell, he surrenders to her power.

It is perhaps interesting to note that from the testimonies of witches tried in Britain in the seventeenth century, we learn that their Sabbath had retained the symbols of transformation of the Muse. It is said that a wizard, the witch's dark god and teacher, would start the ritual of the chase around a magical ring. The order of the chase had been inverted: the Muse used to chase the poet, whereas in the witch's rituals, the man chased the woman, as a result of the patriarchal influence to which even "wise women" were not immune.

The Devil, or wizard, would pursue the female leader of the coven around the ring of witches. She would transform into various beasts, the same as those mentioned for the Muse, quoting an appropriate formula for each transmutation. The man would be expected to adapt his changes to hers. The changes into the various beasts were according to a seasonal sequence, inherited from the original myths of the triple Goddess, protector of the three seasons and of the wild beasts. In England

Left: The appearance of the Muse in one of her myriad of disguises could be felt with a shiver running down the spine, the tearing of the eyes and a sudden chill and stillness in the air. Her essence was at once demonic and inspiring. Above: The nature of the Muse owes her power to the unconscious forces that populate the male psyche.

nowadays, fox and hare hunting still occurs on the days which were celebrated in ancient times as agricultural festivals, and in which odes to the transforming Muse were chanted. [66]

Believing the Impossible Woman

"A man a woman, a woman a man,
Tristan Isolt, Isolt Tristan." [67]

THE poetic literature of the Gothic period was characterized by flight of fantasy through which the spirit of man experienced elevation from the earthly domain to the spiritual and enlightened form of self-annihilation.

The spiritual fire of the "lover" was as nourishing and as fulfilling as prayer, holy bread and wine were for the man of God.

The sensual, ecstatic poetry was developed in countries deeply embedded in the asphyxiating, quasi-pagan, ritual of the Catholic countries. Sacred life in the early Middle Ages was involved with the clerical corpus, the priests, monks and friars, living in closed communal monasteries, far apart from the world. The true nature of the senses was frowned upon by all men of God, who repressed it, mortified their flesh through chastisement in order to kill it and erase it from their spirit. Sensual perception remained therefore a brute and savage force. Nature, in its unconquerable irony, gave the hermit in the woods savage animals as companions, to remind him, ad infinitum, of that which he wanted to conquer.

"Hylas and the Nymphs" by John W. Waterhouse. The nymphs were spirits of nature that could be seen only by the most sensitive of men. The capricious and fickle nymphs took human semblance only to kidnap the man for a year and a day.

The dark world of the Middle Ages was transformed into one that worshipped noble Love in the form of a woman. For the men of God, the priests, there was the socially shared frenzy of the building of thousands of cathedrals and churches. Almost mythically inspired by the Virgin Mother Mary, the leading Muse of the twelfth and thirteenth centuries, people expressed an intensity of conviction which could never again be surpassed by any passion. According to statistics, in the single century between 1170 and 1270, the French built eighty cathedrals and nearly five hundred churches of the cathedral class, which would have cost, according to an estimate made in 1840, more than five thousand million French Francs to replace – equivalent to ten thousand million dollars today. [68]

The soul of the Virgin Mother Mary represented a world of light, purity and utter beauty desired by all. Alongside the mythical cult of Mary, there developed the myth of the Devil, for neither were possible without the other and disbelief in either was, according to catholic doctrine, sinful. The Devil gained possession of human souls and seduced them into heresy, lechery and black-arts. Prayers and hymns of glory dedicated to the Holy Virgin were chanted alongside the cries coming from the pyres on which the damned were being burnt to redeem humanity from the temptation of the Devil. Such a strong belief in Heaven and Hell brought the holy crusades, in which thousands of men, in the service of Christ, conquered the world and forced it into accepting the wisdom of the Catholic Church.

Left: "Stregozzo" by Raimondo Marcantonio. The world of the Middle Ages saw the men of God fighting a fierce battle against the Devil, who gained possession of human souls and seduced them into heresy and lechery. Right: The belief in Heaven and Hell brought the Holy Crusades in which thousands of men in the service of Christ the Savior conquered the world and forced it into Christian belief and conversion.

By contrast with the priests, inspired by the Virgin Mary, the troubadours believed in a new hedonism, which appeared in the poetic expression of the "courtly lovers," in order to re-create life and save it from the rough and arid well it had been thrown into. With the troubadours came the return of virtue, lost in the corruption of nature, through the Fall of Adam and Eve.

Woman became the Muse, the inspirer of noble love and love stories. The end to which her lover attained was not the consummation of the bitter-sweet fruit of love, but the experience of noble love itself, for it elevated his spirit to the radiance of eternal life.

This type of romance represented a challenge to the establishment of the Church, for it proved nobility in corruptible Nature. The themes of the ancient gods and goddesses of nature were thus resurrected in the context of knights in shining armor and genteel damsels. The mythological legend of Isolt and Tristan, reflects all the ideals of Gothic noble Love. Despite the fact that Isolt had been married to King Mark and her love for Tristan was, in fact, adulterous (a mere fact of life!), she represented the pure spirit of woman in that she elevated both herself and her lover to the celestial clarity of intentions.

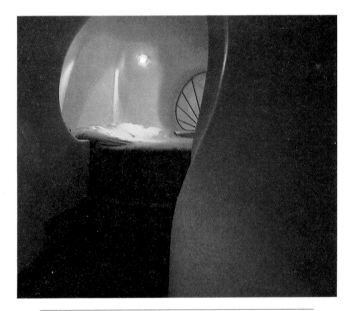

Above: The bed which enclosed the love songs of Tristram and Isolt was hewn in crystal and stood at the center of a room in the "Grotto for the People in Love." Right: The Grotto of the secret lovers was closed by a bronze door inscribed to Love.

The poet Gottfried thus describes the place in which the lovers Tristan and Isolt took refuge from the damsel's sacramental marriage to King Mark:

"The grotto had been hewn in heathen times into the wild mountains, when giants ruled, … And there it had been their wont to hide when they wanted privacy to make love. Indeed, wherever such a grotto was found, it was closed by a door of bronze and inscribed to Love with this name : la fossiture a la gent amant, which is to say, "The Grotto for People in Love."

The name well suited the place. For as its legend lets us know, the grotto was circular, wide, high, and

with upright walls, snow-white, smooth and plain. Above, the vault was finely joined, and on the keystone there was a crown…. The pavement below was of a smooth, shining and rich marble, green as grass. In the center stood a bed, handsomely and cleanly hewn of crystal, high and wide, well raised from the ground, and engraved round about with letters which – according to the legend, proclaimed its dedication to the Goddess of Love. Aloft, in the ceiling of the grotto, three little windows had been cut, through which light fell here and there. And at the place of entrance and departure was a door of bronze.

The circular interior is Simplicity in Love; for Simplicity best beseems Love, which cannot abide any corners; in Love, Malice and Cunning are the corners. The great width is the Power of Love. It is boundless. Height signifies Aspiration, reaching toward the clouds: nothing is too much for it when it strives to rise where the Golden Virtues bind the vault together as the key…

The wall of the grotto is white, smooth, and upright: the character of Integrity. Its luster, uniformly white, must never be colored over; nor should any sort of Suspicion be able to find there bump or dent. The marble floor is Constancy – in its greenness and hardness, which color and surface are most fitting.; for Constancy is ever as freshly green as grass and as level and clear as glass. The bed of Crystalline noble Love, at the center, was rightly consecrated to her name, and right well had the craftsman who carved its crystal recognize her due: for Love indeed must be crystalline, transparent and translucent…."

"The Love grotto represents a magic circle within which the two lovers meet and "they looked upon each other and nourished themselves with that…. Nothing but their state of mind and love did they consummate." [69]

The circle becomes the sanctuary of noble Love, hidden away in the wilderness of the mountains, for true Love cannot be found in the worldly environment, but one must undertake the arduous and dangerous pathways that lead in the innermost recesses of the mountainous caves. Noble Love was the enchantment of the heart, by which the mind was arrested and raised above desire and loathing in the luminous stasis of ecstatic pleasure. The apotheosis of this state was reached by the Florentine poet Dante when he met the eyes of Beatrice and the world came to a stand-still, to pronounce in that silence, the unison of the heartbeat of the two lovers.

"At that instant, I say truly, the spirit of life, which dwells in the most secret chamber of the heart, began to tremble with such violence that it appeared fearfully in the least pulses, and, trembling, said these words : Ecce deus fortior me, qui venient dominabitur mihi (Behold, a god stronger than I, who coming shall rule over me)." [70]

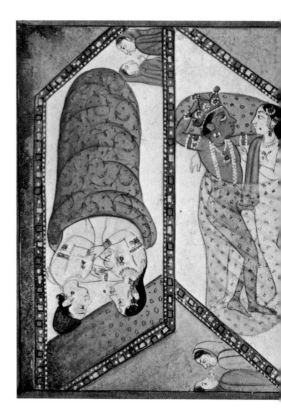

The Divine Comedy unfolded from that instant in which Dante chose Beatrice as his Muse. She was the pure light that led man from the dark abyss of Hell, through Purgatory, to the eternal blissfulness of Paradise.

The poets who sang the virtues of noble Love, such as Dante, Gottfried, and Abelard (in his work

When true love is met in human form the world comes to a stand-still, to pronounce in that silence, the unison of the heartbeat of the two lovers. Below: the Lord Krishna celebrates the power of Love. On the left: A human couple re-enact the divine act of love.

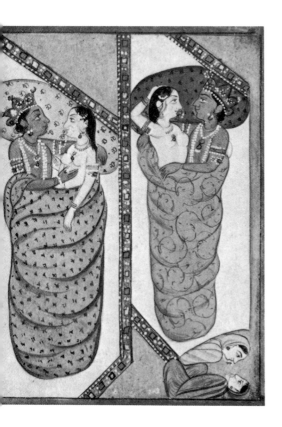

entitled *Heloise*) had the courage to declare openly, after centuries of dark repression of the individual instinct, their knowledge of love. None of them ever denied knowing human love, which was the stepping stone to the sublimation of higher feelings. Their courage was to state against tradition and to expose what stood firm in their own *personal* experience.

The poetic literature of noble Love was developed in other countries as a means to join the human experience, the truest and most secret, to the divine. The Arab countries, for instance, are thought to be the origin of poetic literature which was sung, rather than written, and developed in the verses of the Sufi current of Islam. Important exponents of Sufism inhabited Moorish Spain [*] and from there the tradition was passed on to France, Italy and other European countries, as well as traveling by sea to the Celtic areas of Ireland and Wales.

The songs sung to a woman echoed all the way from Tripoli, Baghdad, Granada, to the courts of the Welsh and Irish kings. Almost at the same time, a similar poetic line was also developed in India in *The Royal Song of Saraha*, which was the founding pillar of the Tantric vision. Saraha, a learned disciple and a descendant of Buddha, leaves all worldly affairs to follow a woman from a lower caste. He attains to enlightenment by uniting his royal destiny with her, and she becomes the medium through which he can taste the divine. In Japan and China we find similar erotic poetry, but everywhere the woman was either aristocratic, a female of inferior caste, a professional courtesan or a slave girl. It is only in the Western development of erotic poetry that we find the producers of such fine literature and the Muses inspiring it, among men and women of *this*, our, world.

The poetry is based on convictions which unfold from the personal experiences of the tellers. The ordinary man becomes thus the myth-maker in modern times, creating myths from ordinary lives. Modern mythology is written in the poems, in the dreams of ordinary men and women, and the Muse is far from dead, for she exists, as she always did, in the sensitivity of men of the heart.

* The main area conquered by the Moors in Spain was Andalucia, the home of flamenco, which is perhaps the last remnant of poetry sung and danced in the name of noble Love.

"A girl stood before him in mid-stream, alone and still, gazing out to sea. She seemed like one whom magic had changed into the likeness of a strange and beautiful seabird. Her long slender bare legs were delicate as a crane's and pure save where an emerald trail of seaweed had fashioned itself as a sign upon the flesh. Her thighs, fuller and soft-hued as ivory, were bared almost to her hips, where the white fringes of her drawers were like feathering of soft white down.

Her slate blue skirts were kilted boldly about her waist and dovetailed behind her. Her bosom was as a bird's, soft and slight, slight and soft as the breast of some dark plumaged dove. But her long fair hair was girlish : and girlish, and touched with the wonder of mortal beauty, her face.

She was alone and still, gazing out to sea; and when she felt his presence and the worship of his eyes her eyes turned to him in quiet sufferance of his gaze, without shame or wantonness. Long, long she suffered his gaze and then quietly withdrew her eyes from his and bent them towards the stream, gently stirring the water with her foot hither and thither. The first faint noise of gently moving water broke the silence, low and faint and whispering, faint as the bells of sleep; hither and thither, hither and thither; and a faint flame trembled on her cheek.

Heavenly God! cried Stephen's soul, in an outburst of profane joy.

He turned away from her suddenly and set off across the strand. His cheeks were aflame; his body was aglow; his limbs were trembling. On and on and on and on he strode, far out over the sands, singing wildly to the sea, crying to greet the advent of the life that had cried to him.

Her image had passed into his soul for ever and no word had broken the holy silence of his ecstasy. Her eyes had called him and his soul had leapt to the call. To live, to err, to fall, to triumph, to recreate life out of life ! A wild angel had appeared to him, the angel of mortal youth and beauty, an envoy from the fair courts of life, to throw open before him in an instant of ecstasy the gates of all the ways of error and glory. On and on and on and on!" (71)

Left: "Beata-Beatrice" by D. G. Rossetti. "A wild angel had appeared to him, the angel of mortal youth and beauty, an envoy from the fair courts of life, to throw open before him in an instant of ecstasy the gates of all the ways of errors and glory."

The Archetype of the Muse

WOMAN MAKES THE perfect Muse, for her very being, her nature is the artist's inspiration. The Muse woman leads a double life: on the superficial plane she obeys the rules of conventional relating between the sexes. In her heart, however, she is a rebel and seeks to release herself from convention in order to be inundated by the wave of her instincts. When she becomes a purely instinctual creature she is able to attract men, without being personally involved, and to hold their total atten-

tion. When she allows herself to act purely according to her instincts, without her reason interfering in what she says and does, she becomes irresistible to men. For the instinct is led by the moon, which affects both women and men, with the difference that man is her slave and woman is her master, equal to the moon in nature.

The Muse woman is auto-erotic, she entices men not because she is in love with them, but because she seeks to be adored through gaining power over their hearts. Such women steal away the soul of a man, while they themselves remain as cold and unattached as the darkness of the waning moon. They may, however, disguise their coldness with a warm blanket of concern and personal manner. They may appear to know exactly how to care for the man they have chosen and they may believe themselves to be in love with him, remaining unaware of the power game which they are playing beneath the surface.

The Muse woman is not an individual with awareness of herself. She incarnates a spirit of nature for she is purely instinctual. The more personally detached she is in the situation, the more she can plunge into the current of instinct. She is then able to *become* the personification of the man's wishes. It is as if she took every hint he gave her to make herself what he wants. In doing so she creates a strange bondage between the man and herself, for he will feel he cannot live without her, he has become dependent on her reflecting his feminine self. She can then gain power over his heart to fulfill her vanity. A classical situation of this can be seen in couples in which the man utterly adores his wife and cannot be without her, whilst the woman appears cold and dominating. [72]

The femininity of the Muse woman is expressed only when there are men around her, for otherwise she is a cold and dull creature. Their attention lights her with the rare flame of vanity.

The symbol of the Muse woman is the Moon, for the moon mirrors mankind's fears and wishes and holds a dark power over them. The Muse woman could be portrayed with a mirror in her hand, for she is in love with her own image which she shapes according to the man's nature, thus becoming also his mirror. Her nature is that of reflection: she is no one, only becoming through her own reflection in the presence of a man.

Actors are endowed with the gift of the Muse for

they are able to incarnate a dream, making the non-real appear as real.

As long as the Muse archetype is the only one working in a woman's psyche, she will appear as non-human. It is only when the power of other archetypes seize her psyche that she finds release from the terrible force of the waning moon.

Epilogue

Active Archetypes in Everyday Life

THE feminine nature is cyclic and has been compared since the most remote historical times to the different phases of the moon. A woman may therefore feel, within her monthly cycle, the intuitive power within her grow toward fulfillment from the beginning of the cycle to ovulation, and wane toward introspection from ovulation to menstruation.

The ebbing and flowing, however, is not only felt within a month, but also from sexual maturity, which is marked at the onset of the menstrual cycle, to menopause.

Woman's responses to the outer world are influenced and to a great extent generated by her changes within. She is like a breath of fresh air in the fixed patriarchal orientation of life, for she responds with renewed freshness to each event as it is presented to her.

A woman is like a seed containing the potential for the growth of a plant, showing wisdom in her early years and living youthfully later in life. The archetypes described in the different myths can therefore apply to any one given moment in her life. A woman may be maternal like Hera, as determined as Artemis and as seducing as Salome. In her youth she may side with the virgin archetype and feel in tune through her psychic and physical growth with the myths that derived from the virgin Goddess. All this is possible without being in conflict with the multi-dimensions of her psyche, for each trait is expressed in different moments. Body and mind are united in the psychology of the feminine, influencing each other endlessly.

The beauty of a woman is her potential for many dimensions, embracing in her way of being the nuances of many archetypes at once, and perhaps constantly confusing those in the world of a more "rational" propensity!

The Question of Individuality

The love that stems from the understanding of oneself has a transformative power in the psyche. It is as if patterns that had perhaps been misunderstood and repressed suddenly "clicked" into place' and the effort needed in their suppression becomes thus tranformed into harmonious energy pervading the entire personality. In this fundamental process, woman gives herself the chance to be born again as a being of light, as a child of moonlight.

Every woman has the birthright to find out who she is, to strip culturally imposed roles and unveil her own mystery. It is, therefore, very important that the archetypes revealed by the myths should not be adopted as yet another rule to follow, as yet another imposition. Each archetype hints, points the finger at the core of our own nature, which is waiting to express its unique song.

"Judgement of Paris", *15th Century miniature.*

Acknowledgments

I wish to thank all those who have helped me to complete this book. In particular :
Philip Dunn, for his great love, immensity of vision and for his patience in teaching me to write English over the years.
Magda Valine, for weaving magic around the visual contents of the book.
Barbara Gess, my editor, for her great support and gentle guidance toward the completion of the work.
Caroline Herter, for first suggesting the idea to me.
Christine Tomasino for her enthusiasm and deep friendship.
Sandra Sabatini for showing me the silence that exists within the body and the mind.
And finally, I give my thanks to *Osho*, whose enlightened vision and infinite love, have taught me, in silence, more about my femininity than any other man.

PHOTOGRAPHS: Scala, Istituto Fotografico, Florence: 2, 113, 119, 134, 156, 174, 182/3, 186/7, 192, 195, 202, 206, 209, 224, 235. Fatik Album, Turkey: 50/51. Priya Mookerjee, New York: 17. Galleria Uffizi, Florence: 24/25, 85, 122/3, 149. Labyrinth Photolibrary, Florence: 10/11, 13, 18/19, 26/27, 35, 38, 41, 47, 48/49, 52/53, 58/59, 64, 70/71, 72, 75, 92/93, 94/5, 102/3, 104/6/7, 111, 120, 121, 134/5, 157/8, 178/9, 180/1, 189, 207, 208, 212/3, 210/1, 218/9, 220/1, 226/7, 232/3. National Museum, Athens: 28/29. Sulbinkian Foundation, Lisbon: 30/31. Tate Gallery, London: 43, 13. Muséé d'Antiquité, Bordeaux: 45. National Gallery, Parma: 57. Atkins Museum, Missouri: 67. Mihrar K. Serailias: 73. Museum der Bilden den Kunst, Lipsin: 96. Palazzo de' Schifanoia, Ferrara: 124/5. Louvre, Paris: 132. Artwork Magda Valine: 22, 81, 62/63, 78/79, 10/11, 114/5, 146/7, 190/1, 214/5.

Bibliography

(1) C.G. Jung and C. Kerenyi, *Essays on a Science of Mythology. The Myth of the Divine Child and The Mysteries of Eleusis*, Bollingen Series, Princeton University Press, New York, 1969.

(2) Bronislaw Malinowski, *Myth in Primitive Psychology*, The New Science Series, I, New York, and Psyche Miniatures, General Series, 6, London, 1926.

(3) *Man and His Symbols*, edited and with an introduction by C.G. Jung, Aldous Books Ltd., London, 1964.

(4) Joseph Campbell, *The Masks of God : Primitive Mythology*, Penguin Books Ltd., Harmondsworth, 1985.

(5) M. Esther Harding, *Woman's Mysteries – Ancient and Modern, A Psychological Interpretation of the Feminine Principle as Portrayed in Myth, Story and Dreams*, Perennial Library, Harper & Row Publishers, New York, 1971.

(6) Ibid.

(7) Jalaluddin Rumi, *Unseen Rain*

(8) C.G. Jung, *Contributions to Analytical Psychology*, trans. by H.G. and C.F. Baynes (New York and London, 1928), to appear in the *Collected Works*, vol.8, in a revised version as *On Psychic Energy*, Pantheon Books, New York, and Routledge and Kegan Paul Ltd., London.

(9) Ajit Mookerjee, *Kali. The Feminine Force*, Destiny Books, New York, 1988.

(10) Barbara G. Walker, *The Woman's Encyclopedia of Myths and Secrets*, Harper & Row Publishers, San Francisco, 1983.

(11) Penelope Shuttle and Peter Redgrove, *The Wise Wound: Menstruation and Every Woman*, Victor Gollancz, London, 1978.

(12) Paula Weideger, *Female Cycles*, The Women's Press, London, 1978.

(13) Barbara G. Walker, *The Woman's Encyclopedia of Myths and Secrets*, Harper & Row Publishers, San Francisco, 1983.

(14) Anne Bancroft, *Origins of the Sacred. The Spiritual Journey in Western Tradition*, Arkana Paperbacks, Routledge & Kegan Paul Ltd., London, 1987.

(15) Mircea Eliade, *A History of Religious Ideas*, vol. 1, *From the Stone Age to the Eleusian Mysteries*, Collins, London, 1979.

(16) Jean Piaget, *The Child's Conception of the World*, Harcourt, Brace & Company, New York, 1929.

(17) Design Book, Baudrillard quote.

(18) C.G. Jung, *Four Archetypes. Mother-Rebirth-Spirit – Trickster*, Ark Paperbacks, Routledge, London, 1985.

(19) Lao Tsu, *Tao Te Ching*, A New Translation by Gia-Fu Feng and jane English, Wildwood House Ltd., Aldershot, 1988.

(20) Barbara G. Walker, *The Woman's Encyclopedia of Myths and Secrets*, Harper & Row Publishers, San Francisco, 1983.

(21) Leo Frobenius, *Monumenta Africana, Erlebte Erdteile*, Bd. VI.

(22) Marie-Louise Von Franz, *The Process of Individuation*, in *Man and His Symbols*, edited and with an introduction by C.G. Jung, Aldous Books Ltd., London, 1964.

(23) Robert Graves, *The White Goddess*, Farrar, Strauss and Giroux, New York, 1948. In "The Single Poetic Theme," pages 440 et sequim.

(24) Ibid.

(25) Robert Graves, *The Greek Myths*, vol.I, Penguin Books Ltd., Harmondsworth, 1960.

(26) Ibid.

(27) M. Esther Harding, *Woman's Mysteries – Ancient and Modern. A Psychological Interpretation of the Feminine Principle as portrayed in Myth, Story and Dreams*, Perennial Library, Harper & Row Publishers, New York, 1976.

(28) Ajit Mookerjee, *Kali. The Feminine Force*, Destiny Books, New York, 1988.

(29) Ibid.

(30) Erich Neumann, *The Great Mother. An Analysis of the Archetype*, translated by Ralph Manheim, Bollingen Series XLVII, Princeton University Press, Princeton, 1963.

(31) Robert Graves, *The Greek Myths*, Vol.2, Penguin Books Ltd., Harmondsworth, 1960.

(32) Isak Dinesen, *Anectotes of Destiny and Ehrengard*, Vintage Books, Random House Inc., New York, 1985.

(33) Karl Kerenyi, *Goddesses of Sun and Moon*, translated from German by Murray Stein, Spring Publications Inc., Dallas, 1979

(34)+(35)+(36) Ibid.

(37) Barbara G. Walker, *The Woman's Encyclopedia of Myths and Secrets*, Harper & Row Publishers, San Francisco, 1983.

(38) Robert Graves, *The Greek Myths*, Vol.1, Penguin Books Ltd., Harmondsworth, 1960.

(39) Ibid.

(40) Ibid.

(41) Barbara G. Walker, *The Woman's Encyclopedia of Myths and Secrets*, Harper & Row Publishers, San Francisco, 1983.

(42) Jonas Hans, *The Gnostic Religion*, Beacon Press, Boston, 1963.

(43) Mary Daly, *Beyond God the Father*, Beacon Press, Boston, 1973.

(44) Marija Gimbutas, *The Goddesses and Gods of Old Europe. Myths and Cult Images.*, Thames and Hudson Ltd., London, 1982.

(45) Sir James George Frazer, *The Golden Bough. A Study in Magic and Religion*, Collier Books, Macmillan Publishing Company, New York, 1963.

(46) M. Esther Harding, *Woman's Mysteries – Ancient and Modern. A Psychological Interpretation of the Feminine Principle as Portrayed in Myth, Story and Dreams*, Perennial Library, Harper & Row Publishers, New York, 1976.

(47) Lucius Apuleius, *The Golden Ass*, translated by W. Adlington, Book XI.

(48) Sir James George Frazer, *The Golden Bough. A Study in Magic and Religion*, Collier Books, New York, 1963.

(49) M. Esther Harding, *Woman's Mysteries – Ancient and Modern. A Psychological Interpretation of the Feminine Principle as Portrayed in Myth, Story and Dreams*, Perennial Library, Harper & Row Publishers, New York, 1976.

(50) Sir James George Frazer, *The Golden Bough. A Study in Magic and Religion*, Collier Books, New York, 1963.

(51) Ibid.

(52) Jean Shinoda Bolen, *Goddesses in Everywoman. A New Psychology of Women*, Harper & Row Publishers, New York, 1984.

(53) Sir James George Frazer, *The Golden Bough. A Study in Magic and Religion*, Collier Books, Macmillan Publishing Company, New York, 1963.

(54) Barbara G. Walker, *The Woman's Encyclopedia of Myths and Secrets*, Harper & Row Publishers, San Francisco, 1983.

(55) C.G. Jung, *Four Archetypes. Mother-Rebirth-Spirit-Trickster*, Ark paperbacks, Routledge, London, 1988.

(56) Frederick Leboyer, *Le Sacre de' la Naissance*, Le Seuil, Paris.

(57) Joseph Campbell, *The Masks of God : Primitive Mythology*, Penguin Books, Harmondsworth, 1969.

(58) M. Esther Harding, *Woman's Mysteries – Ancient and Modern. A Psychological Interpretation of the Feminine Principle as Portrayed in Myth, Story and Dreams*, Perennial Library, Harper & Row Publishers, New York, 1976.

(59) Sir James George Frazer, *The Golden Bough. A Study in Magic and Religion*, Collier Books, Macmillan Publishing Company, New York, 1963.

(60) M. Esther Harding, *Woman's Mysteries – Ancient and Modern. A Psychological Interpretation of the Feminine Principle as Portrayed in Myth, Story and Dreams*, Perennial Library, Harper & Row Publishers, New York, 1976.

(61) *Man and His Symbols*, edited and with an introduction by C.G. Jung, Aldous Books Ltd., London, 1964.

(62) Robert Graves, *The White Goddess*, Farrar, Strauss and Giroux, New York, 1948.

(63) Ibid.

(64) Barbara G. Walker, *The Woman's Encyclopedia of Myths and Secrets*, Harper & Row Publishers, San Francisco, 1983.

(65) Robert Graves, *The White Goddess*, Farrar, Strauss and Giroux, New York, 1948.

(66) Ibid.

(67) Joseph Campbell, *The Masks of God : Creative Mythology*, Viking Penguin Inc., New York, 1968.

(68) Ibid.

(69) Ibid.

(70) Dante Alighieri, *Paradiso XXXIII*. 1-21. Translation by Charles Eliot Norton, *The Divine Comedy* of Dante Alighieri, Houghton Mifflin Co., Boston and New York, 1902.

(71) James Joyce, *A Portrait of the Artist as a Young man*, Jonathan Cape Ltd., London, 1916.

(72) M. Esther Harding, *Woman's Mysteries – Ancient and Modern. A Psychological Interpretation of the Feminine Principle as Portrayed in Myth, Story and Dreams*, Perennial Library, Harper & Row Publishers, New York, 1976.